RESEARCH AND PRACTICE IN SOCIAL STUDIES SERIES

Wayne Journell, *Series Editor*

Place-Based Social Studies Education: Learning From Flint, Michigan
ANNIE MCMAHON WHITLOCK

Teaching Villainification in Social Studies:
Pedagogies to Deepen Understanding of Social Evils
CATHRYN VAN KESSEL AND KIMBERLY EDMONDSON, EDS.

Civic Engagement in Communities of Color:
Pedagogy for Learning and Life in a More Expansive Democracy
KRISTEN E. DUNCAN, ED.

Developing Historical Thinkers: Supporting Historical Inquiry for All Students
BRUCE A. LESH

Toward a Stranger and More Posthuman Social Studies
BRETTON A. VARGA, TIMOTHY MONREAL, & REBECCA C. CHRIST, EDS.

Critical Race Theory and Social Studies Futures:
From the Nightmare of Racial Realism to Dreaming Out Loud
AMANDA E. VICKERY & NOREEN NASEEM RODRÍGUEZ, EDS.

How to Confront Climate Denial: Literacy, Social Studies, and Climate Change
JAMES S. DAMICO & MARK C. BAILDON

Racial Literacies and Social Studies: Curriculum, Instruction, and Learning
LAGARRETT J. KING, ED.

Making Classroom Discussions Work:
Methods for Quality Dialogue in the Social Studies
JANE C. LO, ED.

Teaching Difficult Histories in Difficult Times: Stories of Practice
LAUREN MCARTHUR HARRIS, MAIA SHEPPARD, & SARA A. LEVY, EDS.

Post-Pandemic Social Studies:
How COVID-19 Has Changed the World and How We Teach
WAYNE JOURNELL, ED.

Teaching History for Justice: Centering Activism in Students' Study of the Past
CHRISTOPHER C. MARTELL & KAYLENE M. STEVENS

Place-Based Social Studies Education

Learning From Flint, Michigan

Annie McMahon Whitlock

Foreword by Mona Munroe-Younis

TEACHERS COLLEGE PRESS
TEACHERS COLLEGE | COLUMBIA UNIVERSITY
NEW YORK AND LONDON

Published by Teachers College Press,® 1234 Amsterdam Avenue, New York, NY 10027

Copyright © 2024 by Teachers College, Columbia University

Front cover by adam bohannon design. Photo by Jacob Boomsma / Shutterstock.

All rights reserved. No part of this publication may be reproduced or transmitted in any form or by any means, electronic or mechanical, including photocopy, or any information storage and retrieval system, without permission from the publisher. For reprint permission and other subsidiary rights requests, please contact Teachers College Press, Rights Dept.: tcpressrights@tc.columbia.edu

Library of Congress Cataloging-in-Publication Data

Names: Whitlock, Annie McMahon, 1981- author.
Title: Place-based social studies education : learning from Flint, Michigan / Annie McMahon Whitlock.
Description: New York, NY : Teachers College Press, 2024. | Series: Research and practice in social studies series | Includes bibliographical references and index. | Summary: "Whitlock scrutinizes the Flint water crisis to drive critical inquiry in the classroom, and to show how the curriculum can propel social change. It offers key "takeaways" to help educators apply place-based education in Pre-K-16 classrooms"— Provided by publisher.
Identifiers: LCCN 2023031628 (print) | LCCN 2023031629 (ebook) | ISBN 9780807769744 (paperback) | ISBN 9780807769751 (hardcover) | ISBN 9780807782415 (ebook)
Subjects: LCSH: Social sciences—Study and teaching (Elementary)—United States. | Social sciences—Study and teaching (Secondary)—United States. | Social sciences—Study and teaching—Methodology. | Place based education—United States. | Drinking water—Contamination—Michigan—Flint. | Flint (Mich.)—Social conditions—Study and teaching.
Classification: LCC LB1584 .W4884 2024 (print) | LCC LB1584 (ebook) | DDC 300.710973—dc23/eng/20230814
LC record available at https://lccn.loc.gov/2023031628
LC ebook record available at https://lccn.loc.gov/2023031629

ISBN 978-0-8077-6974-4 (paper)
ISBN 978-0-8077-6975-1 (hardcover)
ISBN 978-0-8077-8241-5 (ebook)

Printed on acid-free paper
Manufactured in the United States of America

For Maggie. Always.

Contents

Foreword	xiii
Preface	xv
Introduction: How Did We Get Here?	1
When Did the Water Crisis Start?	3
Piecing It Together	5
When Everyone Learned About Flint	7
Dealing With It	9
Social Studies and Critical Place-Based Education	10
Are We Finished Yet?	11

PART I: HOW CAN SCHOOLS RESPOND TO A COMMUNITY'S NEEDS?

1. A History of Innovative Education in Flint	15
Manley and Mott: The Brains and the Bank	16
Flint as the Leader in Community Schools	16
Schools and Society	18
Looking Back to Look Ahead	19
Learning From Flint: Critical Place Historical Inquiry in the Classroom	20
2. Why Flint? Teaching Conditions Amidst the Water Crisis	23
The "Preloaded Distributional Injustices" of Flint	24
Built With the Community in Mind	26

	Beyond "Normal": Teaching at Freeman	27
	Learning From Flint: Critical Place Inquiry in Geography	30
3.	**An Uncertain Future for Education in Flint**	**33**
	Community Schools Today	34
	Integrated Student Supports	35
	Extended Learning Time and Opportunities	38
	Family and Community Engagement	39
	Collaborative Leadership and Practices	41
	Learning From Flint: Place-Based School Improvement	43

PART II: HOW CAN SCHOOLING BE REIMAGINED TO CENTER "PLACE"?

4.	**Designing Early Childhood Education in Flint**	**47**
	Early Childhood Education and Lead Poisoning	48
	Childcare in Formal Settings	52
	Using Human-Centered Design to Respond to Early Childhood Needs	54
	Learning From Flint: Designing Place-Based Education	57
5.	**Reggio-Inspired Education in Flint**	**59**
	Reggio Emilia as Place-Based Education	60
	Building Place-Consciousness in a Reggio Toddler Classroom	62
	Preschoolers' Narratives of Flint	67
	Understanding Reggio as Social Studies Inquiry	71
	Learning From Flint: A Call to Research and Practice	73
6.	**Montessori for Flint**	**77**
	Montessori's Connections to Place-Based Education	78
	The Benefits of a Public Montessori Education	79
	Challenges for Public Montessori	81
	Montessori for Flint	83
	Learning From Flint: Incorporating Montessori Elements	86

7. **Flint's Place-Based Charter School**	**89**
School of Choice in Flint	91
Flint Cultural Center: A Longtime Gem	92
Flint Cultural Center Academy	93
A Day at the Flint Cultural Center Academy	95
Learning From Flint: Schoolwide Place-Based Education	98

PART III: HOW CAN TEACHER PREPARATION BE PLACE-BASED?

8. **Place-Based Teacher Education in Flint**	**103**
Place-Based Teacher Education	105
Uniquely Flint	107
Co-Teaching	110
School Culture Shock	112
Partnering With Beecher Community Schools	114
PBTE and Water Crisis Connections	116
Learning From Flint: Literally	118
9. **Place-Based Social Studies Methods in Flint**	**121**
Place-Based Social Studies Methods	122
Elementary Social Studies Methods in Flint	124
Field Trips	127
Right Under Our Noses	130
Teaching Critical Geography	133
Learning From Flint: Transforming Into Place-Based Teachers	134

PART IV: WHERE DO WE GO FROM HERE?

10. **What I Learned From Flint**	**139**
What I Learned About Flint	140
What I Learned From Flint About Place-Based Education in Social Studies	142

What I Learned From Flint About Myself	143
Conclusion	144

References 145

Index 157

About the Author 167

Place-Based
Social Studies Education

Foreword

At the start of the Flint water crisis in 2014, I had the distinct pleasure of working closely with Annie McMahon Whitlock through the "Teaching for Equity" teaching circle at the University of Michigan-Flint. We and other teacher educators came together to study how to devise place-based educational experiences that would prepare future teachers to teach and learn from students of all races and backgrounds with love, cultural humility, and self-reflection—including the ways one moves through the world with privilege. Our goal was to prepare the next generation of teachers to create systemically inclusive classrooms and schools so that children in any school district will thrive through a culture of belonging and community engagement. I participated as a UM-Flint staff member building a system of support (i.e., professional development, technical assistance for equitable service-learning partnerships, and funding) for community-engaged faculty and students and their community partners. Faculty participants in the teaching circle were kindred spirits, committed to building on community assets while extending the resources and impact of the university to uplift people, neighborhoods, schools, and organizations in Flint and the surrounding area.

When getting to know Annie during the teaching circle, I found her to be astutely tuned into the needs and struggles of both youth and future teachers. As echoed through this book, she helped create a culture of vulnerability, inquiry, and reflection on our perspectives and practices, including within the context of larger institutional structures like the university and local school systems. This enabled teaching circle participants to unpack the transformational social changes needed within teacher education that would build strong relationships between teachers and P–12 students. Her passion for students, social studies education, learning through self-reflection, and systems thinking was clear and contagious!

In 2015 Annie and I became new moms and our firstborn children both had a difficult start to their lives. As Flint residents, my son suffered from a severe eczema rash covering nearly every inch of his body from bathing in the water (while I similarly developed the autoimmune disorder psoriasis), at a time when public officials assured Flint residents that the water was safe for bathing. In this book, Annie shares her personal story of her daughter Maggie's difficult entrance into this world after drinking Flint water during her pregnancy (before officials declared a state of emergency) and the educational support Maggie and other children need to mitigate the harm caused by the Flint water crisis. Our heart-wrenching experiences as mothers and educators forced us to closely examine the forces that shape our lives—the systems, policies, and underlying racism that created and continually reinforce stark socio-economic and environmental health disparities.

After the teaching circle, Annie and I took on new roles to put our lessons to work in the spirit of preventing suffering for youth in the future. I served as the liaison between the Flint community and the U-M School of Public Health in Ann Arbor for the Flint water crisis response, then founded a nonprofit, the Environmental Transformation Movement of Flint (ETM Flint), to grow environmental justice champions and a powerful collective movement for environmental health equity in Flint. Annie wrote this unique book, expertly weaving together personal storytelling, archival and interview research, and her firsthand knowledge as a teacher educator. With a keen ability to formulate incisive questions, she presents strategies for place-based critical inquiry through the lens of Flint and the Flint water crisis but which are applicable anywhere.

I found this book absolutely riveting. Although I have learned about Flint history and power dynamics through 17 years of community organizing and public service roles, Annie synthesizes multiple sources of inquiry in a way I've not seen before. Much has been written about the Flint water crisis, but this is the first synthesis of Flint history and the water crisis through the lens of educational systems and how social forces construct a sense of place that influences the lives of students, preservice teachers, teachers, and parents. Just as a pedestrian moves through and experiences their surroundings differently than a driver does, Annie shows readers how to slow down and be present in their lived experiences defined by place and their relative power and privilege in it.

This book analyzes what is and has been, as well as what could be and how to get there. *Place-Based Social Studies Education: Learning From Flint, Michigan* is a practical and accessible, yet complexly insightful read. Whether you are a social studies teacher, teacher educator, place-based/community-based instructor, history buff, social justice champion, or Flintstone, this book is for you.

—Mona Munroe-Younis
Executive Director
Environmental Transformation Movement of Flint

Preface

Learning social studies in Flint, Michigan, or really anywhere, is rooted in the concept of place. *Place* is often referenced as one of the five themes of geography, and in that sense the concept of place is often taught with a focus on cultural and human geography as a way to describe a location (Gersmehl, 2014). But place is more than a description, and certainly the city of Flint is more than how people describe it. Creswell (2004) writes that place is a "rich and complicated interplay of people and the environment" and a "way of knowing" as much as it is a "thing in the world" (p. 19). Social studies as an interdisciplinary school subject is also a way of knowing and can also be described as a complicated interplay of people and environment highlighted by a focus on inquiry within social studies education. Place is essential to inquiry and social studies.

I came to work as an education professor in Flint in 2013, most of my time there overlapping with the Flint water crisis, an ongoing event in which residents of Flint suffered lead poisoning through their water supply because of government negligence. Prior to working in Flint, I danced around other connected topics to place-based education, including inquiry, civic engagement, and project-based learning. But as I worked in the city and through my experiences with the water crisis, my own development as a scholar became place-based.

Creswell (2004) also writes that "when it comes to place, life is fieldwork. The world itself is the best kind of resource for thinking about place. An observant geographer can learn a lot about place by reflecting on their everyday experience" (p. 127). In 2016, I became a social studies syllabus come-to-life, but I fumbled my way through trying to contextualize the water crisis for my own students, who were very much living it right there with me. My goal for this book is that it becomes what I wish I had for myself back in 2016. If something doesn't exist, write it yourself, right? I want readers to come away understanding that place-based education in social studies is more than geography; it is a way of knowing that requires a critical reflection of the interplay of one's environment with the people in the community as well as oneself (Creswell, 2004).

Each part of this book highlights critical place inquiry (Tuck & McKenzie, 2015) and place-based education with an overall inquiry question. Each individual chapter investigates this question by examining Flint—and the Flint water crisis, more specifically. This book is a large narrative inquiry, featuring interviews from several Flint residents involved in education in the city—from school officials to teachers to parents to teacher educators. These experiences can mirror how a social studies educator might approach understanding their own places. In the spirit of "life is fieldwork," this book also allows me to reflect on my own experiences of learning from Flint in relation to my positionality as a white, cisgender female who lives outside of the city.

In Part I, I investigate the question, *How can schools respond to a community's needs?* I use a critical place methodology to examine the past, present, and future of Flint Community Schools and suggest ways to study history and geography from a local, place-based perspective in social studies. Flint Community Schools once was a leader in the community schools movement and seen as a shining example for the success of public schooling in America. I provide historical analysis from a critical place perspective and the possibilities of studying place-based local history in classrooms. I also examine the immediate response from Flint Community Schools to the water crisis, as many of the city's schools were directly impacted. Understanding how lead in the water disproportionately affected schools in the city requires an understanding of spatial injustices in connection to the historical analysis. I also discuss the possible future for Flint Community Schools specifically, including the overlapping traumas of the Flint water crisis and the COVID-19 pandemic. As many other urban centers around the country are dealing with infrastructure issues exacerbated by the COVID-19 pandemic, Chapter 3 touches on arguments for a more place-based approach to school improvement.

In Part II, I consider a question I thought quite a bit about when envisioning how education would/could change as a result of the water crisis in Flint: *How can schooling be reimagined to center "place?"* In light of schools rapidly switching to virtual learning, to face to face, and back again during the pandemic, this question is asked frequently. Educators and parents in Flint have been investigating this question long before COVID in thinking about how to best meet the needs of students impacted by lead poisoning. This section highlights how different educational entities in the city have adapted their approach to education given the specific place they are in, including public, private, and home childcare, Reggio schools, access to Montessori education, and a place-based charter school. The section explores what these educational groups are doing in the city to create education models rooted in Flint.

In Part III, I look inward to investigate the question, *How can teacher preparation be place-based?* Here I examine the commitment to place-based teacher education at the University of Michigan-Flint, where I worked as a teacher educator. I reflect on the opportunities and challenges to making system-wide changes to be more place-based, as well as modifications I made to my own teaching and course design as a response to the water crisis. I use this section to describe my choice to incorporate more place-based elements in my social studies methods courses.

Finally, in Part IV, I look at this idea of lessons from Flint by asking simply, *What did we learn?* and *What's next?* This concluding section circles back to a discussion of place-based social studies education and social studies teacher education. I argue that place-based education helps us to understand our communities better, which in turn makes us better social studies educators because we can take action within our communities when we can listen and learn from them. The example of the Flint water crisis, though highly specific to Flint, isn't entirely unique, and lessons can be learned about the opportunities and challenges to place-based education from this context. In many ways, we don't fully know what's next for Flint, and we are still processing the lessons we've learned.

This book would not have been possible without the help of numerous Flint residents and educators who shared their stories and their work for this project. These include Jim Ananich, Marissa Cobleigh, Jen Cozart, Harold Ford, Shamarion Grace, Elizabeth Jordan, Sharneese Jones, Suzanne Knight, Jeff Kupperman, Heather Laube, Eric Lieske, Amanda Ling, Carolyn Miller, Jordan Munerlyn, Toko Oshio, Jodi Ramos, Jacquie Richardson, Starletta Rett-Henry, and Hana Sankari.

Many people also influenced, and continue to influence, my place-based work and/or helped me to research and conceptualize this book. These include Thomn Bell, Mary Black, Callum Carr, Liz Cunningham, Danielle De La Mare, Aviva Dorfman, Samantha Engel, Jing Fu, Mona Hanna-Attisha, Linda Heck, Thomas Henthorn, Andrew Highsmith, Christine Kenney, Joslyn Marinelli, Carrie Mattern, Sara McDonnell, Laura McLeman, Mona Munroe-Younis, Ben Pauli, Maria Salinas, Karen Salvador, Leyla Sanker, Lance Sumpter, Katy Swalwell, Sapna Thwaite, Jan Worth-Nelson, and all of my Flint students. I also appreciate Kristy Brugar, Brenniss Carncs-Ferguson, Wayne Journell, and my dad, Mitch McMahon, for giving me feedback on drafts of this book. I am forever thankful to Mike, Maggie, and McKenzie Whitlock for being my support, my joy, and my cheerleaders.

I continue to be influenced by people and places in Flint that are special to me. Among many examples are the University of Michigan-Flint, Flint Farmers' Market, various murals of the Flint Public Art Project, the Flint Community Read, Comma Bookstore, Reclaimed by Whaley, the Whaley House, the Stockton House, the Ferris Wheel Building, Café Rhema, and the South Parks neighborhood. The lessons I learned from these places are infinite.

Place-Based
Social Studies Education

Introduction
How Did We Get Here?

In the fall of 2019, I slipped into a late afternoon lecture on the campus of the University of Michigan-Flint, where I worked as an education professor. Dr. Ben Pauli had been invited to speak by the Political Science Department, and since I was preparing to write about my Flint water crisis journey and Dr. Pauli had recently released his book about his experiences (*Flint Fights Back: Environmental Justice and Democracy in the Flint Water Crisis*), I thought his lecture would be helpful. Dr. Pauli is a sociologist at nearby Kettering University, an engineering school in Flint. (Admittedly I was also curious about humanities professors at science and technology-focused schools, but that's a sidetrack.) I grabbed a donut and sat down, passing the Flint Registry table set up there to track Flint residents affected by the crisis and connect them with help. *I really need to sign up for that*, I thought, as I made my way to my seat.

Dr. Pauli began his talk with an overarching theme from his book about perspectives. When did the water crisis start? Who gets to decide when it's over? As he discussed the different historical, technical, and political perspectives that make up the varied answers to these questions, I began to consider how I would answer these questions. When did the water crisis start for me? Is it over? For an educator, will the crisis ever be over? It's these questions that sparked this book.

As Dr. Pauli discussed his positionality as a relatively new Flint resident who had moved to the city at the beginning of the water crisis, I reflected on my own position as an "outsider." I am a white, cisgender woman, which makes me part of the dominant group in many communities, but not in Flint, which has a majority Black population (United States Census Bureau, n.d.b). Many Flint residents past and present take pride in the shared experience of being a "Flintstone." I have never lived in Flint, which means I don't have that shared history. As an "outsider" in this way, I experienced the water crisis in very different ways than did the Black residents of the city. I do have a deep attachment to Flint. I spent more time there than I did in my home most weeks, especially during a semester. My daughters came to daycare with me on our campus in Flint, and we frequented the city on weekends as a family. I'm a teacher educator who worked in elementary schools in Flint and was faced with challenges in my work caused by the water crisis—challenges I had never experienced before.

I have lived my whole life in the state of Michigan, but I didn't grow up near Flint. My husband did, though—in Lapeer, Michigan, about 15 miles east of Flint. In the summer of 2000, when we started dating, I would drive through Flint on my way to visit him. Before those drives on I-69, my only other exposure to Flint was through stories of population decline from General Motors, the failed AutoWorld, and Michael Moore. I was initially surprised to learn—13 years later, when I began working at the University of Michigan-Flint—how little my husband knew about the city despite living so close. After learning more about the community, I could see how if one lived 15 miles away, they might as well be 100 miles away.

But the first time I stepped foot in Flint, in 2013, I was instantly smitten. To this day, I remember the feelings I had while touring the UM-Flint campus on a snowy March day during my job interview, buying coffee on Saginaw Street the day I signed my hiring paperwork, and overlooking the city from the top of the Northbank Center during a meeting in my first fall semester. To me, the city felt like a small town—everyone seemed to know each other and where they went to high school. The residents I met in that first year were educators and entrepreneurs (I had done some research in economics education right before I came to Flint) who were committed to building the city back again. The comeback narrative was strong, and it felt good to think I might possibly contribute to that.

I considered my first year as an education professor at UM-Flint a success. I had met a lot of new people, and despite living an hour from campus in metro Detroit at the time, I felt committed to the city's growth. I was looking for ways to get involved with the Imagine Flint Master Plan, a document outlining a 20-year improvement strategy for the city. Adopted in October of 2013, the plan had sections connecting education, economic development, and housing, among others, and its developers were looking to faculty at UM-Flint to connect to the implementation of the plan. Some of my colleagues and I were redesigning our secondary teacher preparation programs to be more place-based and community-focused, and to find ways to get our students involved in the implementation of the comprehensive master plan. I finished my first year excited about the future.

I remember leaving campus one evening after teaching my social studies methods course and seeing signs around the parking garage and spray painted near the manhole covers in the street. The signs were alerting people to the upcoming scheduled switch to the Flint River water as the main source of water for the city—warning people that this was a terrible idea. This was noteworthy to me not only because this was the first I had heard of this particular issue, but having just come from teaching about youth activism and civic engagement in my social studies methods class, I had the history of the city's activism on my mind. I remember thinking this was where I was meant to be—in a city that lived and breathed *social studies*. I thought to myself, *I should read up on this water thing. Would I have time this semester to talk about it in class?* I didn't talk about it that semester, after all. But I would definitely get my chance again.

WHEN DID THE WATER CRISIS START?

During finals week at the end of my first year at UM-Flint, the city switched its river water source from Lake Huron to the Flint River. The date of April 25, 2014, is considered by many to be the "first day" of the Flint water crisis. Regarding civil suits, statutes of limitations, and acknowledging "anniversaries," April 25, 2014, is a day people will remember in Flint. However, the start of the Flint water crisis is not so black and white.

Andrew Highsmith, a historian who completed his dissertation on the history of Flint at the University of Michigan in Ann Arbor, wrote a book widely read among Flint residents called *Demolition Means Progress: Flint, Michigan and the Fate of the American Metropolis (2015)*. In his book, Highsmith describes how industrialization and racial segregation led to the city's dwindling population in the early 2000s. His book is an in-depth historical analysis of the impact of segregation on the public school system and housing in the city, going back to the early 20th century. Although the book was published right before the water crisis news broke nationally, and thus doesn't mention the crisis specifically, the path leading to the water crisis is nicely outlined.

Highsmith writes of Flint's history with "administrative segregation" (p. 8) of redlining and gerrymandering school districts to maintain racial separation in the city. As the suburbs surrounding Flint incorporated themselves, and therefore created their own taxable wealth and utilities, Flint became essentially "landlocked" and unable to grow. This suburb separation explains why my husband, who grew up in one of these suburbs, seldom visited Flint. Flint residents also have a history of concern over environmental issues. The construction of I-475 caused upheaval in primarily Black neighborhoods, evicting people from their homes and pushing them into public housing. For residents in the North End of Flint, the water crisis wasn't even their first experience fighting against lead poisoning. In the 1990s, North End residents fought the Michigan Department of Environmental Quality over the Genesee Power Station, which was releasing lead-toxic fumes into the air (Highsmith, 2015). Ultimately, the plant was able to continue running, but this example has echoes of the water crisis. Many Flint residents live where they live for reasons in which they had little say. The poor infrastructure that exists in these spaces is not an accident. The comeback narrative for the city, preceding the water crisis, focused on rebuilding the downtown area as opposed to upgrading blighted neighborhoods or funding a school system dealing with fewer resources as a result of a smaller tax base. This explains why I could eat dinner at an upscale wine bar in downtown Flint during my job interview, and later drive by rundown houses right up against I-475 on my way home. Highsmith's book describes how the conditions in Flint were prime for what was to come. The water crisis perhaps began 100 years prior to switching the water source to the Flint River.

One of the resulting effects of Flint's population decline and financial instability, as outlined by Highsmith, was that Flint was put under control of an "emergency financial manager" in 2011. Pauli (2019) and many other activists in Flint cite Michigan's Emergency Manager Laws of 2011 as the "start" of the water crisis—a full three years before the water switch. Governor Rick Snyder was elected in 2010 as the "tough nerd," a venture capitalist who promised financial solutions and a perspective differing from those of the "career politicians" he ran against. At the time, facing an imminent bankruptcy from the city of Detroit, Snyder's business solutions appealed to many Michiganders. In 2011, Snyder passed Public Act (PA) 4—the "Emergency Manager law"—proposing that Emergency Managers (EMs) could be appointed by the state to take over municipalities and school districts in the state that were financially unstable. EMs could overrule elected officials on all financial decisions, essentially rendering the rule of the people null and void. Flint was immediately assigned an EM in late 2011, creating furor among residents who felt they were being stripped of their democratic power.

Prior to 2014, Flint had received its water from the Detroit Water and Sewage Department (DWSD), which pumped water from Lake Huron an hour north to Flint at a significant cost. Flint EMs Mike Brown and later Ed Kurtz signed a contract connecting Flint to the Karegnondi Water Authority (KWA), a group of regional municipalities that were building a pipeline directly east to Lake Huron so they could access this water at less expense and treat it at the city level. While the pipeline was being built, the city would use water from the Flint River. Although the Flint City Council voted in agreement to this, EM Kurtz had the authority to join the KWA under the Emergency Manager law, so the council's vote was merely "symbolic" and "not binding" (Bebow, 2016, p. 28).

By April 2014, as the city prepared to make the switch to Flint River water, resident activists were trying to persuade others that this wasn't a wise decision. Pauli writes in his book that it was popular lore around Flint that the river was a "repository for shopping carts, old cars, and the occasional corpse" (2019, p. 1). It was also known that the river and the adjacent Thread Lake were not safe to swim in or eat fish from. I worked on a project for one of my courses in 2015 with the South Parks Neighborhood Association, a group concerned with water quality for years before the official switch of the city's drinking water. The common narrative outside of

Flint was that residents became concerned with water quality after lead was found in their drinking water, but this was not when concerns began.

PIECING IT TOGETHER

In April 2014, the official water switch was made. Less than 3 weeks later, residents were complaining about rashes on their skin and emailing the Environmental Protection Agency (EPA) and the Michigan drinking water liaisons there (Bebow, 2016). As people bought bottled water and activists set up a water relief site (Pauli, 2019), government officials were telling people that the water was safe to drink, they just needed to get used to the new water source, and they were "wasting their precious money buying bottled water," to quote Dayne Walling, Flint's mayor at the time (Bebow, 2016, p. 37).

In the summer of 2014, I became pregnant with my oldest daughter Maggie. Although I lived an hour away from Flint at the time, I spent some time in the city working throughout that summer and returned to campus for the fall semester, joyfully announcing my pregnancy to my colleagues and students. Pregnancy had made me incredibly thirsty all the time. I was drinking more water than ever before, as a tall glass of ice water was the only thing that kept me from throwing up on most days. I regularly drank water when I taught classes, and at that time I was refilling my water bottle many times a day from a fountain near my office. On some days, the water came out opaque white and bubbling; I would dump it out and find another fountain with clearer water, which I would then drink. One day, I showed a colleague the weird color of the water from that first fountain, and his comment was familiar: "I think it's fine. We just have a new water source we have to get used to." At the beginning of that fall semester, we received three "all faculty emails" regarding the boil water advisories in Flint. We were instructed not to drink the water for a few days. I would then waddle my pregnant self down the hall to a water cooler to refill my water bottle. When the boil advisory lifted, I returned to my closer fountain.

Then, in October 2014, the GM plant in Flint announced they were not going to be using city water in their engine plant because the water was corroding the engines. This news was met with some alarm among city residents I spoke with about the safety of Flint water. "If it's corroding car engines, how can we safely drink it?" The Michigan Department of Environmental Quality (MDEQ), via an interview with MLive's Ron Fonger, is quoted as saying "[the MDEQ should not be] branding Flint's water as 'corrosive' from a public health standpoint simply because it does not meet a manufacturing facility's limit" (Bebow, 2016, p. 38). In other words, cars were more important than people. That month, I stopped using the water fountain closest to my office, and haven't used it since. In fact, it's no longer there.

In March of 2015, I gave birth to Maggie Jaymes Whitlock, a beautiful girl who started life on the wrong foot. After unexpected and unpredictable complications during delivery, she spent several minutes without oxygen to her brain, resulting in permanent brain damage. I spent the first half of 2015 in a fog of trauma, stress, and uncertainty, searching for an explanation for what had happened to my daughter. I didn't visit Flint once in 6 months, spending most of my time away from work and sleeping in an NICU waiting room in Detroit. As I was disconnected from my "normal life," mothers in Flint were similarly dealing with trauma, stress, and uncertainty. Their children were exhibiting behaviors unfamiliar to them: getting sick, developing rashes, losing their hair. These mothers were not quiet, sharing their concerns with any public official who would listen; their emails and phone calls were routinely dismissed. In fact, on March 3, 2015, as my daughter entered this world, Flint's EM Jerry Ambrose reported to the Michigan Department of Treasury that returning the city to DWSD would have "extremely negative financial consequences" and that "the water provided to Flint users today is within all MDEQ and EPA guidelines" (Bebow, 2016, p. 63).

It took several months for my daughter to recover enough for us to bring her home from the hospital, and for me to feel comfortable with returning to work in Flint. I was eager to get back to working with the community on the Imagine Flint plan, and I was excited about doing a project with my class with the South Parks Neighborhood about revitalizing the Thread Lake area. I had missed Flint. I missed my work and felt ready to escape my fog.

I taught my next class in the fall of 2015 and had not yet connected the dots from the water switch protests and boil water advisories of 2014 to what was about to happen. The class I taught in our secondary education program was called "Community, Family, Self." The main objective of the class was to examine the intersections of place and education, using a definition of place as part of the self and the family unit in addition to a physical location. My students and I worked with the South Parks neighborhood, interviewing residents, walking the area, and mapping the community's assets.

During one particular discussion about access to basic utilities and needs within a community as an asset, the subject of water access came up. I knew of Flint's rising water cost due to population loss, and my students shared stories about high water bills. One student then made a seemingly flippant remark that stopped me: "Yeah, and we can't even drink it. It's all brown. It's basically poison." Other students nodded in agreement. I was taken aback. Almost instantly, his comment connected a million little bits of data that had been stored up in my brain for 18 months. The spray-painted manhole covers. The opaque water from my drinking fountain. The boil water advisories. At home that night, I searched for the story of Flint water. My timing couldn't have been more serendipitous. Just a couple weeks earlier, Dr. Mona Hanna-Attisha had discovered an increase in lead levels in

Flint's children. These increases corresponded to the April 25, 2014, switch to the Flint River water.

WHEN EVERYONE LEARNED ABOUT FLINT

The year 2016 was an unforgettable period of my career. The study conducted by Dr. Hanna-Attisha (or "Dr. Mona," as she is lovingly called in Flint) opened up the rest of the world to what had been going on in Flint since the water switch. Since I had been in a fog of being a new mother to a baby with intense medical needs, I had missed important information, which I was now discovering along with the rest of the world. Not every water complaint by Flint residents in 2015 went unnoticed. Miguel Del Toral from the EPA, upon investigating a complaint from Flint resident Lee Ann Walters, discovered an inconsistency with the water sampling process that obscured data that would show high levels of lead in Flint water. Walters had contacted Marc Edwards, a professor at Virginia Tech who had researched lead levels in water in Washington, DC. Edwards and a team of researchers traveled to Flint to take water samples in early 2015, and instructed Walters on how to take her own water samples. She then canvassed the city, spearheading a massive water sample collection for Edwards to analyze. The result confirmed Del Toral's findings—lead levels in Flint water were extremely high. Combined with Dr. Mona's data on how these lead levels were impacting children, by early 2016 the story was out there. Flint's water was not safe to drink. Children were being harmed. The state government knew of the issue but did nothing to help.

Working in Flint during a time when the city was on everyone's mind was a surreal experience. I couldn't walk to my office without passing news vans parked along the street, shooting B-roll footage or interviews in front of my building. It was not uncommon for people to share celebrity sightings around the city, as famous people flocked to Flint to hold charity events or manage donations. "A Concert for Flint," performed at the Whiting Auditorium and featuring numerous musicians, actors, and other entertainers, was a benefit for Flint livestreamed out to the world (Hinds, 2016). Bottles of water were everywhere. Our campus childcare center became a hub for collecting water for families, and hundreds of cases of bottled water lined the hallways for families to take (see Figure 1.1). President Obama visited Flint, famously drinking the water in May 2016 (Korte, 2016). Since 2016 was a presidential election year, Flint also saw visits from Senator Bernie Sanders, Secretary Hillary Clinton, President Bill Clinton, and then presidential candidate Donald Trump. The democratic primary debate in March 2016 was held in Flint, also at the Whiting Auditorium. Our campus turned into a base camp for journalists as our Rec Center and library were broadcast stations, disrupting campus life for our students.

Figure 1.1. *Water Bottles Line the Hallways of the Early Childhood Development Center at UM-Flint*

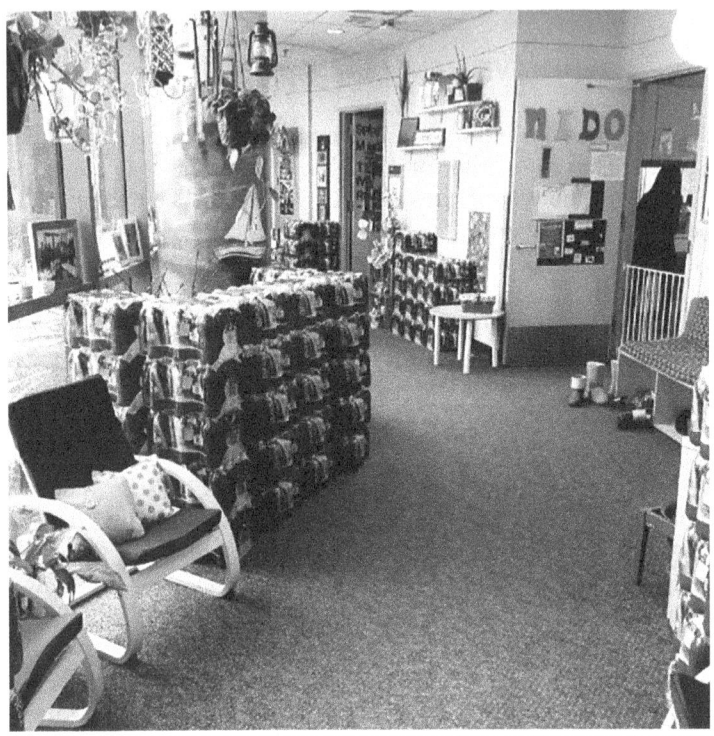

The influx of people, attention, and water bottles seemed like a nuisance to my students. As a social studies professor, I tried to engage my teacher candidates in issues of environmental racism and civic activism that were happening around us, literally, every day. They expressed fatigue—they were tired of dealing with the water and then coming to class to talk about it. As my colleagues in Flint and in the greater social studies community expressed how "easy" it must be to teach social studies and place-based education at that time, I couldn't help but feel I was missing something. My students didn't want to talk about any of it.

One day, an educator with expertise in working with young children exposed to lead paint came to speak to several elementary education classes. Lead exposure has been a problem for children long before the Flint water crisis, as children exposed to lead-based paint in older houses frequently exhibited health issues that school leaders had to work with. After his presentation on the seriousness of what lead exposure can do to the human brain during the crucial developmental weeks, months, and years of a child's life, the large group listening sat in silence. There was no going back to our regularly scheduled syllabi. The student teachers working in a Flint elementary school asked me questions about what they were supposed to do next. Other students expressed fear about drinking the water, afraid their brains, or their children's brains, had been damaged. We were all "piecing together" the possible known and unknown ramifications of our actions and were contemplating where to go from here. I was right there with them, with no answers or experience to share. For an academic whose life's work is sharing "answers" and "experience," this was jarring to say the least.

In that moment, and for several months after, none of my students wanted to discuss the historical and political events and decisions that led Flint to the water crisis. In that moment, fear, uncertainty, and anger bubbled to the surface. One student said most frustrating for her was that in a few months Flint would be just another news story. "Everyone will forget about us, but we'll be left to deal with it." How we're "dealing with it" is essentially the theme of this book. And in many ways, her prediction was accurate.

DEALING WITH IT

Governor Snyder declared the water crisis "over" when the city switched back to the DWDA, and then declared it "over" again when the state stopped handing out water bottles to Flint residents in 2018. Celebrities stopped coming. When Snyder's term expired, Governor Gretchen Whitmer was elected, and her administration gave Flint residents hope that Snyder and others would be prosecuted for their role in the water crisis. It took until January 2021, but charges were finally brought against several individuals, including Emergency Managers Darnell Ealy and Jerry Ambrose and Governor Snyder. But many residents were disappointed to learn that Governor Snyder was only charged with two misdemeanors for his neglectful role (House, 2021); they were more disappointed when those charges were dropped in 2022 (Watson & Musa, 2022). Flint residents were awarded $641 million in damages in 2020, most of it earmarked for legal fees, special education services, and children under 6 (Gustafson, 2023), but money can't fully address what has been done to the city.

I am writing these words after 3 years marked by another national health tragedy—the COVID-19 pandemic. COVID-19 disrupted everything, including schooling all over the country. As I was set to write a book about how education in Flint has been impacted by the water crisis, it's now difficult to separate what is an impact of the water and what is the impact of the pandemic. It's difficult to separate because the water crisis is very much ongoing in Flint. Many homes and neighborhoods remain in the process of having their pipes replaced, a process paused during the height of the pandemic.

It's very hard to wash your hands to prevent the spread of disease when you don't have clean water, or any water at all, as many Flint residents had their water shut off due to delinquent bills (National Resource Defense Council, 2020). Many residents, like my student in my "Community, Family, Self" class, simply refused to pay large amounts of money for poisoned water. Genesee County, where Flint is located, became a hotbed of COVID cases in April of 2020, and again in October of that year (Roth, 2020). Some side effects of the water crisis have been exacerbated by the COVID-19 pandemic.

SOCIAL STUDIES AND CRITICAL PLACE-BASED EDUCATION

It didn't take me long to recognize the social studies lessons in the Flint water crisis. I tried to work them into my classes from the first time I saw the literal warning signs posted on my parking garage. Good social studies instruction in schools or in teacher preparation programs is taught through questions—through inquiry. Social studies is also interdisciplinary. The National Council for the Social Studies (NCSS) defines social studies as comprising history, geography, civics, economics, sociology, other humanities, as well as relevant content from science and mathematics (NCSS, 2008). Inquiry instruction involves using knowledge of these interconnected disciplines to investigate questions, evaluate sources of knowledge, and take action with this knowledge. After some time to reflect, I can see the inquiry questions forming more clearly.

In place-based education, the community is an extension of the classroom. Important concepts, content, and constructs are all contextualized for students through the lens of the local. Sobel describes this as "pedagogy of place" (2005, p. 11), where the school and community are intertwined, the community looking to students as valuable resources for change, and the school curriculum giving students space to be agents for change. Place-based education is connected to inquiry-based learning and project-based learning, approaches that are used to engage students in the community as part of school. The Flint water crisis made it essential that my teacher candidates understand the complex interplay of people and environment that inform how they teach social studies. For me as an educator, the water crisis accelerated my own reflection on place. The more I learned about Flint, the more I realized that we all might learn not from just the water crisis, but the city itself, as an example of how to engage in place-based social studies.

For example, studying the geography-based inquiry question *Why do people live where they do?* can lead students to learning about people migrating to certain Flint neighborhoods in the 1930s, and then the history of redlining in the city and activists fighting for open housing, which all had an impact on the areas of the city most affected by the water crisis. Studying civics questions such as *Should elected officials always make every decision for their constituents?* helps us understand how the local government, the state government, and the national government and governmental agencies failed Flint when it came to clean water, and how those levels of government are (or aren't) taking responsibility to rectify it. This, of course, would have to involve a discussion of the EM law, which many argue started the water crisis. Even examining a public issue question such as *Should we have to pay for water?* can lead to discussions of water shutoffs during a global pandemic and whether those violate basic human rights. These are critical place inquiry questions (Tuck & McKenzie, 2015) that educators in any place can use to make meaning of their world and experiences through studying both the spatial injustices in a place and resistance to injustices.

Highsmith quotes General Motors historian Carl Crow in his book as saying, "America is a thousand Flints" (2015, p. 23). He was referring to the progress of the auto era and the mentality of the city as a symbol of prosperity. Now, I feel the expression takes on a new meaning. Much has been written about the water crisis and its potential health and environmental impacts (Clark, 2018; Hanna-Attisha, 2018; Pauli, 2019), but only years removed from the initial hit in 2014, can we really begin to understand its long-term effects, particularly on education. As the young children who were babies or in utero in 2014–2015 became kindergartners, was the Flint school system prepared to meet their education needs? How has education changed in the city as a response to the water crisis? Or hasn't it? Do teacher educators in the city, like myself, have a responsibility to educate our candidates differently considering the crisis? And since Flint, and the United States, and the world are looking at education differently in light of the COVID-19 pandemic, what lessons can we learn from these overlapping traumatic events?

ARE WE FINISHED YET?

"Place is not simply something to be observed, researched, and written about but is itself part of the way we see, research, and write" (Creswell, 2004, p. 25). The fundamental concept of place-based education is that place becomes a part of how and what one learns as well. *Where* one learns social studies or learns to teach is just as integral a part as *what* one learns or *how*. This quote by Creswell speaks to me because Flint has become a part of how I see, think, parent, research, write, and study social studies. I write about place-based education through the Flint water crisis because that is how I see the world now (Gruenewald, 2003a). Of course, other places have similar stories we can learn from as well.

The overarching inquiry of this book is based on a simple question that I first heard Dr. Pauli ask the room during his lecture that fall day: *Is the water crisis over?* His argument was that it depends on who is answering the question. This book is my answer to the question: It's not over. Educators and education professionals in Flint have much more work to do, and it's not close to being finished. I feel that, years later, I can finally start to wrap my head around studying what happened to me, to my students, and to their students, and how Flint became my fieldwork.

Part I

HOW CAN SCHOOLS RESPOND TO A COMMUNITY'S NEEDS?

CHAPTER 1

A History of Innovative Education in Flint

I spent a considerable amount of time talking to Flint residents over the 9 years I worked in Flint. One thing you notice when talking to people who grew up in Flint is that everyone seems to know everyone else. Having grown up in a small farm town in west Michigan, I am familiar with this phenomenon, as the town I grew up in had more cows than people. Flint is an urban center, topping out at close to 200,000 people in 1960 (Thorne, 2014). It's not possible for literally everybody to know everybody, but people in Flint greet strangers as if they grew up together. Part of why I find Flint so charming is that it reminds me of where I grew up—with way fewer cows.

The idea of "community" appears frequently in social studies standards in Michigan and in other states. "Community" is a collection of people unified by common characteristics in a physical space, but community is also a feeling of unification and togetherness. However, communities can also be exclusionary and reflect power dynamics (Choi, 2002). Understanding the complexity of community requires attention to intersectionality (Crenshaw, 1991)—a community is more than the sum of its parts. Byker and colleagues (2018) defined community as "the contextual intersection of culture, economy, history, location, which reflects how groups of people associate with each other" (p. 162).

A deep sense of community runs through Flint, a sense that everyone is connected in some way. When I listen to residents talk to each other like old friends, they bring up what elementary or high school they went to, what sports they played, and what "programs" they participated in. School and sports as a connector of community isn't unique to Flint, but there is a very specific history in Flint underlying the shared sense of community. Engaging in a place-based historical analysis of a community can help make connections for teachers about the context in which they're working and where their students are living. In Flint, when residents talk about the "good old days" when the public school system was one of the best in the country, it's not just exaggeration and hometown pride (well, maybe a little). The historical roots to such a statement help to explain how Flint residents came to feel these connections and how important they are to understanding place.

This chapter takes a historical look at schooling in Flint and how schools helped build—and divide—community in Flint. Understanding this history not only helps us to comprehend the roots of the Flint water crisis but can also serve as a model on how to help students understand how any place came to be the way it is.

MANLEY AND MOTT: THE BRAINS AND THE BANK

In 1935, deep in the middle of the Great Depression, a physical education teacher in Flint named Frank Manley spoke to the Flint Rotary Club. He presented his idea for more after-school programming for the youth of Flint, a need he felt would combat juvenile delinquency and crime. His ideas for a "boy's club" involved organized sports and recreation that could also be available for unemployed adults looking for something to occupy their time (Decker, 1999). Attending that Rotary Club meeting was Charles Stewart (C. S.) Mott, one of the richest men in Flint (and the United States) at the time, with a net worth of over $800 million. By 1935, C. S. Mott had amassed a fortune in the wheel and axle business, as he moved to Flint just in time to capitalize on the invention and manufacture of the automobile. He was on the board of directors for General Motors, and by 1935 had already served three terms as the mayor of Flint and run as a Michigan Republican gubernatorial candidate (in 1920).

C. S. Mott established the C. S. Mott Foundation in 1926, an initiative that began by funding the Flint Institute of Arts and other charitable interests of the Mott family. Over tennis at his Applewood Estate, Mott agreed to give Manley $6,000 for his "boy's club," under the suggestion that he use already-existing school buildings to house his programs (Krajewski & Osowski, 1997). From that point on, Manley and Mott developed a partnership that drastically altered the future of education in Flint. The Mott Foundation became the primary bankroll for Frank Manley's vision for community schools—an idea bigger than just "keeping the lights on."

FLINT AS THE LEADER IN COMMUNITY SCHOOLS

With financial backing behind him, Frank Manley envisioned a school system in Flint that was the center of the community and took the lead on solving social problems in the city (Decker & Romney, 1992). He developed the role of a Community Schools Director, who would be the liaison between the neighborhood, the school, and the community program, using advice from Community Councils and Block Clubs so that residents were driving the programming based on their needs. This developed into educational practices that continue to this day all over the country, such as police liaison officers (now featured prominently in schools, for better or for worse) (Ryan et al., 2018), free breakfast for children made by volunteer mothers in the community, and home counselors to reach out to families in need (Decker, 1999). Manley understood the connections between the health of a community and the health of the school, speaking to the integration here, as cited in Decker (1999):

> We found out that everything is so interrelated, physical health, mental health, emotional health, education, the curriculum, the teaching, the family, the everyday living, and so on, so that you can't pull them apart and say that any one segment is going to take care of these social ills. So, I thought the best chance we might have is if we brought all these forces together ... As soon as you get one community started and they begin to believe in each other and have a better understanding, then you can spread that out in a little wider circle. ... (p. 28)

This quote from Manley refers to the concept of *place* in a sense that he is understanding the complicated integration of people and environment that Creswell (2004) describes and the intersectionality of community (Byker et al., 2018). As the community schools movement in Flint expanded in size and influence, the Mott Foundation became an integral part of this complicated integration.

The community schools movement in Flint was funded entirely through the Mott Foundation. They were seen as a charitable group working through structures that were already in place to fund what the community needed. In 1947, Manley wrote that the Mott Foundation simply "greased the wheels of existing machinery" (Flint Public Schools Can Be the Best, 1951), essentially giving the foundation credit for making the school system and neighborhood groups work better. As paternalistic as that sounds, it's hard to ignore the positive influence of the foundation on the community of Flint. By the 1950s, Flint had expanded offerings for adult education, an "Interracial Community Center," and summer camps open to "all races, classes, and creeds" (Flint Public Schools Can Be the Best, 1951). Evidence indicates that educators in Flint were also in favor of community schools. At a workshop in 1953, teachers were encouraged to be public relations agents for the model, and Flint hosted workshops on how to replicate Flint's model (Manley's model) of community schools in other places.

In the 1950s and 1960s, the community schools movement became synonymous with after-school programs for children and adult education programs for their parents and other community members, and the Mott Foundation became synonymous with community schools. By 1970, 90,000 Flint residents were engaged in 1,300 community education courses (Campbell, 1972, p. 195), called the "Mott Program." The foundation worked through the Flint Public School Board of Education by providing money to the board for the programming. However, the concept of "community schools" was still very separate from the day-to-day educational experiences happening in schools. Education in Flint operated as two separate systems—the K–12 system with a superintendent of schools, and the after-school community programming that had its own superintendent for community education (Decker, 1999)—and in many ways, the Mott Foundation controlled both.

SCHOOLS AND SOCIETY

The concept of intertwining school and life outside of school had long been a focus of Progressive Era educators such as John Dewey and William Heard Kilpatrick. In 1902, Dewey wrote of the role of the teacher in exposing children to subject matter in service of developing children's interests and connecting their education to their real life. In his University of Chicago Lab School, students worked on hands-on tasks that had authentic connections to their community. Kilpatrick's "project method" (1918) developed from Dewey's philosophies. In his project method, Kilpatrick believed that students should be learning through solving practical problems within the community. The foundations of place-based education stems from these Progressive Era philosophies as well. In good place-based experiences, not only does the school, classroom, or students provide what a community needs, the students also learn from the community through engaging in educational experiences in that community. Place-based education sees the city as the extension of the classroom as a valuable place of learning for students (Schmidt, 2007).

Manley's model for community education in Flint was in line with the view that the city of Flint would be an extension of the classroom, but mostly to let others into the life of the school, rather than to introduce students to the life of the community. From the 1940s to the 1970s, students in Flint were engaged in the community through "extension" experiences that were managed separately from the educational experiences in the school. For example, instead of students engaging in civic action projects that might positively impact the community (Kilpatrick's "project method"), students were going after school to an organized basketball program also open to other community members. Both are educative experiences, but in very different ways that need not be mutually exclusive. However, in the literature on Frank Manley's community model, the focus is on the benefits that the community gets from developing the school system into a community center (Decker & Romney, 1992); it is harder to find literature on Manley and Mott's community schools model that references anything happening in K–12 classrooms at the time (Decker & Romney, 1992).

Frank Manley saw this separation of "education" and "community education" and attempted to remedy it, successfully convincing the board of education to go down to one superintendent (Decker & Romney, 1992). The Mott Foundation trusted the Flint Public School Board to distribute Mott Foundation money to fund community schools. But the separation was there, and there it remains to this day.

LOOKING BACK TO LOOK AHEAD

Exploring Flint today reveals that C. S. Mott and his descendants remain omnipresent in the city. One can walk down Kearsley Street and attend classes at Mott Community College, and then go tour his Applewood Estate nearby. The Mott Foundation and the Ruth Mott Foundation fund activities in Flint and around the world that focus on supporting and building community in areas of education and environmental sustainability (Charles Stewart Mott Foundation, 2023; Ruth Mott Foundation, 2021). With the reach of C. S. Mott all over Flint, it would be easy to submit to heroification (Loewen, 2007), regarding Mott as a savior of the city. I'm literally writing these words in a coffeeshop in downtown Flint underneath a painting of the man! However, an understanding of community and education connections in Flint today is incomplete without a more critical historical examination of C. S. Mott and his foundation as a power structure in the city.

Critical race spatial analysis (CRSA) is a methodology that examines the role of racism and white supremacy in perpetuating spatial injustices, particularly in educational systems (Butler & Sinclair, 2020; Morrison et al., 2017). Looking back through the history of community schools in Flint using CRSA intentionally reveals how the Mott Foundation used "community schools" to restrict access to education to students based on race. For example, even the fact that community schooling is attributed to Frank Manley in literature on community schools (Campbell, 1972) ignores counternarratives of neighborhoods that took a community-focused approach to educating children outside of the formal school structures. Quotes from Frank Manley in publications in the 1940s and 1950s explicitly state that community education can "put the Negro on our middle-class level of thinking" (Highsmith, 2015, p. 61). This shows the white saviorism that was an integral part of Flint community schooling.

Andrew Highsmith (2015) wrote extensively on the Mott Foundation's commitment to racial segregation in Flint schools as a key component of their programming. Although the foundation appeared to be committed to racial harmony by opening their programs to children of all races, an abundance of historical evidence reveals that Manley and Mott's programming worked hard to uphold the status quo of racial segregation in Flint in the 1950s. Flint Community Schools opened their first true "community school" in the city in a Black neighborhood, a move that would appear to be helping Black children of Flint gain access to their community services.

However, the programs around that school, Fairview Elementary, were designed to promote vocational training with no access to gifted and talented or college preparatory programs offered in other neighborhoods. The Mott Foundation's hand in the public school system in Flint ensured strict, gerrymandered school district boundaries based on race by allowing white students to transfer out of Black neighborhood schools, but not allowing Black students to transfer to white schools (Highsmith, 2015).

In opposition to Dewey's idea of not training children for a particular career or vocation (1902), the public school system in Flint and the community programming, as a result, steered young Black boys in Flint to be line workers at General Motors (GM)—a convenient source of employment for C. S. Mott, the president of GM at the time. Considering Black GM workers during this time were given the most difficult foundry jobs in GM factories and were often excluded from union benefits from the local Flint UAW due to racism (Highsmith, 2015), this process maintained the status quo of a marginalized Black labor force in the city. Sexism was also entrenched in the connection between GM and education. A document from the 1950s detailing a field trip in Flint schools shows that the boys and girls were split up—the boys visited the Buick plant to "see the automobile put together," while girls visited a luncheon at the Hotel Durant to "develop greater appreciation of attractive table service, manners, and poise."

In 1977, the Mott Foundation suddenly pulled their support of the community schools concept in Flint, taking millions of dollars of school funding with them. Highsmith (2015) said that Mott did this to avoid complying with school desegregation mandates at the time. He writes:

> Mott avoided the harsh language and tactics of [George] Wallace and other demagogues, but his personal commitment to Jim Crow ran deep, and his work in Flint's schools was an outgrowth of his belief that racial segregation was an essential prerequisite for community building and civic unity. (p. 236)

Place-based education has a history in Flint, but it's one rooted in white saviorism and the idea that the (segregated) schools have the duty to fix the community, but that the community has nothing to offer the student. Later chapters in this book describe how many people have worked to alter this state of affairs, but white supremacist structures run deep.

LEARNING FROM FLINT: CRITICAL PLACE HISTORICAL INQUIRY IN THE CLASSROOM

Studying local history or the local community is a regular staple of social studies education, particularly at the elementary level. In the Michigan K–12 Social Studies standards, students in the 2nd and 3rd grades look at the history of their community and the history of Michigan through a lens of Time, Continuity, and Change—heavy on the "Change." Second-graders in Michigan are expected to "explain how individuals and groups have made significant historical changes" and "describe changes in the local community over time" (Michigan Department of Education, 2019). Many standards documents won't overtly mention the continuity of white supremacist structures that are direct ancestors of spatial injustices.

However, the Michigan standards do emphasize using the Inquiry Arc (NCSS, 2013) and the disciplinary processes of historical analysis such as, "use relevant information from multiple credible sources representing a wide range of views, considering the origin, authority, structure, and context, to answer a compelling or supporting question." When this historical analysis comes with an intentional lens to look at oppressive structures, students are engaging in a critical place historical inquiry.

Educators can carefully guide students with sources to examine structures (like the community schools movement) that have influenced current events. Here are some suggestions:

- Look for sources that help students answer the question: *Why is this place the way it is?* You may have to do some of your own digging here, as the Library of Congress most likely will not have historical sources on your local community. I made use of local archivists at the Flint Public Library and on the University of Michigan-Flint campus in the Genesee Historical Collections Center.
- Listen to (and collect) oral histories! Talking to residents is a great way to begin to draw conclusions and see patterns of structural inequity—they lived it (and/or are currently living it). Dr. Erica Britt (2018) has done great work collecting stories of Flint residents through her Vehicle City Voices project. Students can also design their own questions based on their wonderings, practice interviewing skills, and use language arts skills to disseminate their results.
- Frequently reflect on whether you are providing sources that showcase a diverse set of experiences. It was easy to find pieces that hold up Frank Manley's vision of community schools as revolutionary, but less easy to find more critical views. Both are important to understanding local history. Another question would be to ask your students, *why might it be easier to find certain perspectives in a historical analysis than others?*

Uncovering what makes a place the way it is will no doubt uncover multiple truths. The fact that the sense of community in Flint is palpable to an outsider like me could also be a byproduct of the integrated after-school activities from the "Mott Programs." Studying how education in the city has been impacted by the water crisis also uncovered the structures in place within public education in Flint that reinforced and continue to reinforce spatial inequities here. Many of these structures were built by Mott and Manley, for better or for worse. Looking at this history of community schools through a more critical lens unveils a deeper connection between community schools of 1930s Flint with the roots of the water crisis 80 years later—one that suggests that separation, not integration, may have been a more important goal of Manley and Mott's community schools.

CHAPTER 2

Why Flint?
Teaching Conditions Amidst the Water Crisis

"Nobody thought to mention this to us?"

Upon returning to school after the long Labor Day weekend in 2015, 6th-grade teacher Jacquie Richardson walked into the teacher's lounge at Freeman Elementary to find the sinks and coffeemaker taped off. The principal, Anita Steward, explained to the teachers that lead had been found in the school's water supply. A week earlier, local pediatrician Dr. Mona Hanna-Attisha had gone public with her discovery of a spike in high lead levels in children she saw at Hurley Hospital in Flint dating back to April 25, 2014—the day of the switch to using Flint River water. Freeman Elementary School, located off Atherton Road, had welcomed teachers back to school the week before for professional development to start the school year. Jacquie and her colleagues had been drinking the school's tap water out of the drinking fountains. The teachers' lounge coffee had also been made with this same water—where Jacquie grabbed her morning cup. Recounting this memory to me later, Jacquie said nothing about lead had been discussed at Freeman before that point, and this sudden change felt like a betrayal—by whom, she didn't say.

In 2015 and 2016, I spent a lot of time at Freeman Elementary, as Principal Steward had agreed to place seven student teachers and pre-student teachers in her building. As the instructor of the pre-student teaching course (the "apprenticeship") and the student teaching seminar course at the time, I observed my teacher candidates at Freeman as they taught lessons and learned from their mentor teachers (one of them being Jacquie). My visits to Freeman are part of my experience with the water crisis and the place I associate the most with my uncertainty and my own feelings of helplessness.

* * *

But why and how did Freeman get to this point? As a school with one of the highest lead levels in the city in 2015, the conditions at Freeman and many other places in Flint are a result of not just environmental racism but a perfect storm of many other spatial injustices that impacted education in Flint. A critical look at place requires examining the systems that created and uphold these spatial injustices. This is especially important when determining a response to public health crises such as the water crisis or COVID-19 pandemic. This chapter begins by describing some of the systems that led to the water crisis in Flint and how these systems influenced the experiences of two Freeman Elementary teachers at the height of the water crisis: Jacquie, a veteran educator and Flint native familiar with the community schools model from the past, and Hana, a student teacher who was learning about the difficulties of finding the assets in a community among the stress.

THE "PRELOADED DISTRIBUTIONAL INJUSTICES" OF FLINT

In the 1920s, the Flint area was seeing a boom in population of workers coming to General Motors (GM) factories. However, white working-class factory workers were priced out of the city and settled in the surrounding suburbs in hand-built homes. Black residents of Flint were also restricted from housing in the city and limited to certain neighborhoods such as St. John and Floral Park (Highsmith, 2015). By 1933, the housing division of GM created three subdivision housing developments specifically for their workers—their white workers. These new houses had strict racial covenants prohibiting Black people from buying these houses, or even to stay overnight in them unless they were employed by the owners. GM convinced the Flint Board of Education to build two schools for these racially restricted neighborhoods, which also ensured school segregation and housing discrimination would be forever linked in Flint.

By the 1950s, the automotive industry was expanding beyond Michigan, and GM was opening plants across the country in areas with cheaper taxes and less stringent union rules. Because Flint appeared to "not exist without GM" (Highsmith, 2015, p. 130), the city agreed to extend water and sewer usage from the city out to new GM plants in the suburbs of Flint—essentially giving GM access to city resources without paying city taxes and bringing their wealth to suburbs rather than the city. Of course, these new suburbs needed schools. When GM opened a plant in Flint Township, it raised the per-pupil tax funding of the Carman-Ainsworth school district to double that being spent on students in Flint Community Schools (FCS) (Highsmith, 2015, p. 131).

There were several attempts to annex the suburbs into a Flint unified school district and a larger metropolis called "New Flint." The city had no room to expand, and suburbs needed resources from the city, so it seemed a win-win. However, residents of suburbs like Grand Blanc, Flushing, and Swartz Creek were adamantly opposed to annexation. To them, Flint was representative of high crime and poor schools, which may have justified their desire not to be connected to the city. When the focus is on municipalities, utilities, taxes, and city borders (like the arguments against annexation), it can hide the fact that systemic racism created these conditions. The reason not to annex into a New Flint thus "isn't about race" but place and space (Blaisdell, 2017).

These suburbs took it one step further and incorporated themselves into their own municipalities, which made them unable to be annexed according to Michigan law. This essentially cut off the city of Flint from resources, and further codified the separation between the white flight suburbs and FCS. To this day, there are more than seven school districts that border FCS, with six or seven more within 5 or 10 miles (Genesee Intermediate School District, 2023). This doesn't include charter and parochial schools, which all compete for students and resources in Genesee County.

Around the same time as talk of annexation, the city of Flint was debating a proposal from GM to build a freeway interchange in the city for easier access of goods to factories. Many locations for the freeway were considered, but in the end, proximity to downtown and cheaper cost led the state to decide on I-475 being built directly through Floral Park and St. John—primarily Black neighborhoods in Flint. As the government bought up their homes for demolition, Black residents of Flint lost home equity and were displaced to renting homes in public housing (Hayes, 2020; Highsmith, 2015). The decades of the spatial injustices of redlining and freeway construction had made FCS incredibly racially segregated.

In the late 1970s, the discussion of de facto versus de jure school segregation was hotly debated in Michigan. The Flint Board of Education was charged with not doing enough to break up segregation in the city (as demanded by the *Brown v. Board of Education* Supreme Court ruling). This led to years of debates about whether school segregation was just a happenstance result of where people lived or deliberate segregationist policies of school districts near Flint. Of course, where people lived in Flint was not happenstance, as evidenced by racially restrictive housing covenants in GM-built neighborhoods, displacement by the construction of I-475, and even the weather. An F5 tornado ripped through Flint in 1953, causing an upheaval in housing, displacement of residents to public housing, and renewal to rebuild parts of the north end of the city in the Beecher school district (Highsmith, 2012). As a county-wide school desegregation plan was being argued in courts, in 1977 the Mott Foundation abruptly pulled all their funding for community schools and cut off their relationship with Flint Community Schools (Highsmith, 2015), unceremoniously ending the relationship established by C. S. Mott and Frank Manley. Historian Andrew Highsmith argues that the timing of the Mott pullout with the desegregation debate was not coincidental, surmising that the possibility of a massive desegregation effort in Flint was enough to convince the Mott Foundation that they weren't interested in complying.

Redlining, incorporation of suburbs, and freeway construction promoted by GM ensured school segregation in Flint, and the Mott Foundation funded it as long as it stayed that way. When describing empirical research on spatial injustice, Edward Soja (2010) writes that "unjust outcomes arise from inherently unjust processes operating in an urban milieu preloaded with distributional injustices to begin with" (p. 86). The preloaded injustices in Flint led to the unjust processes and outcomes of the water crisis.

By the fall of 2015, the news of lead in Flint water was out there, but somehow wasn't as big a story as it would become. Spatial injustice can explain this as well. As residents were being denied access to fresh water, they were also being ignored as they complained about it. In the eyes of the state and federal government, Flint was not a city they were willing to "go out on a limb" for. Those quotations aren't mine—these words were literally used in an email exchange with Environmental Protection Agency officials about whether to act on information about Flint's water (Burke, 2016). To them, Flint was a place that was economically depressed, being run by an emergency manager, where the elected mayor and city council elected government were considered figureheads only. To the state government, it might seem that lead in the water in Flint was a problem of place and not an immediate problem of systemic racism. However, it wasn't lost on the Black residents of the city that it took Lee Ann Walters, a white woman, and Marc Edwards, a white man, to bring the issue to consciousness (Pauli, 2019).

But even as the issue of lead in the water was being brought to light by residents, scientists, and doctors, many others were actively trying to discredit these people. In October 2015, the *Flint Journal* reported that Freeman Elementary and two other schools had lead in their water supply more than six times the allowable level (Adams, 2015). Even as Governor Snyder was addressing the state and making plans to switch Flint's water supply back to Detroit's water supply, Dr. Eden Wells, Michigan's chief medical executive at the time, still blamed levels of lead in Flint's children on older homes in Flint with lead paint (Hanna-Attisha, 2018). The willful ignorance and denial from power structures about what was going on in Flint is but one of many "unjust processes" related to the water crisis for years to come. On October 17, 2015, inside of the first "true community-type school," city officials held a press conference at Freeman Elementary to announce a reconnection of the city's water supply in Detroit, after 18 months of children and teachers in that school drinking lead-poisoned Flint River water (Fonger, 2015).

BUILT WITH THE COMMUNITY IN MIND

Freeman Elementary was dedicated in 1951 by the Flint Board of Education as "Flint's first true community-type school" (Glasson, 1951, p. 23). Named for Ralph Freeman, a former president of the Flint Board of Education and a federal judge, Freeman Elementary is considered one of the first schools designed as a community school from its initial construction. When you walk into the front door of the school, you enter a lobby with chairs, rugs, and welcoming lighting. To your left is a large auditorium, and across the lobby is a gymnasium. To the right is a hallway that leads to the rest of the school. The first room in the hallway, the only one visible from the lobby, is the "Community Room"—a conference room with a kitchenette and brightly decorated bulletin boards. The hallway continues and takes a turn in an "L" shape where the classrooms are. The main areas that the community would use—the auditorium, gym, and a conference room—are the most accessible and nearly separated from the rest of the school (Decker, 1999).

The 1950s was a period of tremendous growth for community schools in Flint. In addition to Fairview and Freeman Elementary being built for the purpose of community involvement, the Mott Foundation funded more community school directors (Mott Program Upped to $400,000, 1953), created community schools training for other districts looking to emulate Flint's model (Decker, 1999), and put additional teachers, counselors, equipment, and programming in 13 more elementary schools by the end of the decade (Decker, 1999). The Flint School Review publication published an in-depth look at the district's community school offerings in March 1956. At that point, community schools included teen programs, summer camps, weekend activities, adult education courses, health outreach (including a massive campaign for the "Salk vaccine" for polio), and extracurricular classes in art, drama, mechanical skills, and business (including the use of IBM "key punch machines"). It's hard to imagine, considering that in October 2015, 65 years after the building was dedicated to Ralph Freeman, lead levels in the building were six times higher than the allowed limit, and the Atherton Road neighborhood where the school sits had disproportionately high levels of lead compared to other areas of the city (Adams, 2015). However, those 65 years featured a complex interplay of spatial injustices that influenced my experiences with the students and teachers at Freeman Elementary.

BEYOND "NORMAL": TEACHING AT FREEMAN

Jacquie Richardson spent 20 years of her teaching career at Freeman Elementary, starting there in 1998. She remembers that community school directors were still involved in the district when she arrived, and she was excited to be part of what was known at Freeman as "learning communities," where teachers would loop with their students for 2 to 3 years. Jacquie had looped with students in the 4th, 5th, and 6th grades when I met her. Jacquie was a mentor teacher for one of my students in the 2015–2016 school year, but I had heard of her before this. Jacquie was a part of a group called Discovering PLACE—Flint teachers who were committed to place-based education. They attended professional development put on by some of my secondary education colleagues at UM-Flint and received support for their projects from a grant housed in the University Outreach office. In 2015, Jacquie collaborated with another Freeman teacher (and fellow student teaching mentor) and a group called Farm on Wheels to have their students grow vegetables to sell at the Flint Farmers' Market. A lover of history herself, Jacquie is on the board for the Stockton Center, a historical house in Flint once owned by a Civil War colonel. Jacquie frequently took her students there to learn about Flint history and the urban wildlife on the grounds.

In 2015–2016, however, Jacquie's school year was dominated by the water crisis. The central office worked on the immediate need of how to distribute water bottles to school classrooms and to students' families. At Freeman, every water fountain and sink in the building was turned off. Students couldn't even wash their hands after going to the bathroom—the central office supplied the school with hand sanitizer. As water bottle donations began arriving, FCS had to manage all the donations at first—a time-consuming task that involved delivering pallet after pallet of water bottles to every school in the district. Freeman's gymnasium became a storage unit for these pallets, and teachers would need to grab a case of water at the start of each day.

A normal day of teaching for Jacquie that school year involved getting a case of water from the gym in the morning, and taking care to ration it, as the staff received frequent emails from Principal Steward saying that donation deliveries were delayed or that donations had run low. Jacquie then had to find space in her classroom to store cases of water and monitor her trash cans as they overflowed with empty water bottles—there wasn't a place to recycle them. Students' papers were always vaguely damp from condensation on water bottles, and Jacquie constantly had to remind students to put their name on their bottle and to use hand sanitizer when they came out of the bathroom. According to her, it was "one more distraction" when trying to teach, but being without access to fresh water for her students highlighted how much educators rely on it. The possibility of being without water bottles for a day was a real source of anxiety.

In January 2016, another of my students, Hana, had been doing her apprenticeship in a nearby suburb of Davison. Because of staffing issues there, Hana needed a new placement, so she began her student teaching at Freeman in a 1st-grade classroom. Also, in January 2016, it seemed the entire world became aware of what Flint residents had been living with since April of 2014. Mona Hanna-Attisha's research and the local coverage of the crisis was gaining international attention, and soon there was no shortage of water bottle donations.

Having just returned from doing fieldwork in Davison, one of the more rural suburbs of Flint (one that had refused annexation in the 1960s by incorporating), Hana described her entry to Freeman in 2016 as a bit of a culture shock. Kids were frequently absent; she never had a full class of students at one time the entire semester. She noticed rashes on their skin and in their scalps. Hana was worried about exposing herself to lead water. Talking to me later, she didn't recall ever using the bathroom at Freeman Elementary in her 16 weeks of student teaching! She recalled showing the students a YouTube video for a lesson, and a Colgate toothpaste ad played before the video. Students called out in disgust as the woman in the video drank water from her sink and swished it around in her mouth while brushing her teeth. It was clear to Hana that this experience in Freeman would not be the same as her experience in Davison.

Still, there were elements of the community schools concept at Freeman, especially during the water crisis. In the spring of 2016, Freeman put on a school carnival complete with lead testing for families and fresh fruits and vegetables for them to take home. Freeman also gave families water bottles at pickup, keeping the gym open to the public so they could get the water they needed. Similar to Manley's earlier vision, Freeman became the physical hub for community support when it was most needed.

Because of the media attention from the water crisis in 2016, Flint children were seen as victims in the eyes of others. Hana's class received letters and pictures drawn by kids around the world. Hana also saw her students as victims at times. One of the assignments I gave in my student teaching seminar was for my student teachers to write a reflection on the context for learning in their school. This was supposed to be an exploration of the community both inside and outside the school—its assets as well as its challenges. Hana struggled with writing this, and we worked through it together during one seminar time. She was unclear how to write about the water crisis and where it fit in. If these weren't "normal" conditions for the school, how could she write about what it was really like at Freeman? I tried to help her see that these are the current conditions and therefore are very relevant, but I was unsure on how to guide her to thinking about how lead poisoning impacted students. I didn't know that myself at the time.

It was hard for Hana to see the assets of Freeman—every connection with the community was a water crisis response. The whole world was looking at Flint as a deficit, and when you're living that life, it's hard to find the assets that are there. I remember traveling to a work meeting in New York City in 2016 with people around the country. When I said I worked in Flint, you could see the pity in their eyes and the glances at my water bottle. People would always ask if everything was OK, or if I was OK. This would simultaneously frustrate me and make me feel validated. I didn't like being seen as a victim, but I appreciated that people were paying attention to the injustices in Flint.

Flint residents felt similarly about being victimized and found it to be a tricky balance. Residents in Flint were victimized by all levels of government, by emergency managers, by careless environmental agencies. They deserve justice. However, residents struggled with being seen as victims and being defined by what happened to them (Pauli, 2019). In February 2016, a photograph of 2-year-old Sincere Smith taken by a *Detroit Free Press* photographer appeared on the cover of *Time* magazine with the headline "The Poisoning of an American City" and "Toxic water. Sick kids." A sad-looking Sincere is captured with his facial scarring from toxic bathwater. It's a powerful image that shows the gravity of the water crisis but also can reinforce the image that Flint kids are broken and in need of saving. It also reinforces the image that the water crisis is a "place" problem—it's an individual or family issue happening in Flint that came about in 2016. This ignores the systemic spatial injustices that brought Flint to this point.

Hana had a hard time with this too. Student teaching during the height of the water crisis, she said, "made her cry every day." Recalling it to me years later still brought her to tears. Hana was older than a lot of my students and had school-age children who attended a private religious school in the Flint suburb of Swartz Creek. She said she would go home to her own children and remind them of how good they have it and how they have "nothing to complain about" compared to the kids she was teaching. When her student teaching was finished, Hana bought her class erasers and lamented that such a small gift was what they really wanted. She still thought of those 1st-graders as victims, saying, "Does it matter if they learn long division? Does it matter if they catch up? Is it fair to have those high expectations? They have to have their needs met." She reflected on her success, or perceived lack thereof, by saying the water crisis "compounded everything all at once." The "everything" in question—segregation, redlining, poverty, racism—was not yet specific in her mind, but she was able to see that the water crisis was more than a singular event.

LEARNING FROM FLINT: CRITICAL PLACE INQUIRY IN GEOGRAPHY

Two of the five themes of geography are "location" and "place." Location describes where a place is (perhaps by studying maps and representations of places), but place describes what a location is *like*. Who lives there? What are the experiences of the people who live there? What cultural traditions exist there? The integration of location and place is to study *why* places are located where they are and how location influences characteristics of places (Gersmehl, 2014). To examine the influence of place and location more critically, students can look at how systemic spatial injustices such as redlining, freeway construction, and school segregation have clearly had an influence on the lives of those who are affected. Making these issues explicit to students shows how geography has amplified oppression and discrimination (Soja, 2010). This has potential for your students to learn a richer history of a place; critically studying place can uncover counternarratives that can advance equity and justice (Butler & Sinclair, 2020). Flint is not unique in this area—urban centers all around the United States are impacted by one or more of the spatial injustices mentioned in this chapter. Here are some ways that the study of place might advance the pursuits of equity and justice:

- Find a Homeowner's Loan Corporation (HOLC) map of your geographic area (this site can help: https://dsl.richmond.edu/panorama/redlining/#loc=5/39.1/-94.58). Discover what areas in your town were redlined in the 1930s and discuss how these areas might be impacted by this today. Overlay an HOLC map with an issue that means something to you in your community. For example, in Flint, there is a lack of grocery stores in neighborhoods that were redlined—why might this be the case?
- For older students, *Last Week Tonight with John Oliver* did an excellent piece on redlining that helps break down the concept, albeit with some questionable language that may need disclaimers for the classroom (www.youtube.com/watch?v=_-0J49_9lwc). The show *Adam Ruins Everything* also explains redlining quite well and has more classroom-friendly language (www.youtube.com/watch?v=e68CoE70Mk8).
- Continue your examination of local history as described in Chapter 1 by looking for sources that help students answer the question: *Why is this place the way it is?* To help write this chapter, I relied heavily on secondary historical accounts (Andrew Highsmith), which often have helpful analyses, as well as newspaper primary sources. Your local library may have a subscription to archived issues of your local newspaper, as mine did for old issues of *The Flint Journal*.
- Practice applying critical place inquiry when studying other social studies topics. Identify systemic "preloaded" injustices when learning, for example, about global imperialism, development of the U.S. Constitution, or capitalism.
- To avoid the trap of looking at communities from a deficit, create an asset map of your community. Where are places that help people in your community? Where are public green spaces open to everyone? Where can residents go to get healthy food? What neighborhood groups and organizations are organizing for positive change?

The children of Flint were (and continue to be) victims of environmental racism exacerbated by historical spatial injustices in the city. As much as Flint is unique, many urban areas in the United States have similar histories, and perhaps even similar water issues (Mulvihill, 2021). In 2015–2016,

Freeman teachers like Jacquie struggled with the logistics of supplying her students with water and anxiety over the possibility of going without or being poisoned herself from her coffee water. Hana struggled with seeing her students as victims during her student teaching, and was not helped by many people around the world contributing to this narrative as well. But years later, is this story still the same? What remains of the community school model today?

CHAPTER 3

An Uncertain Future for Education in Flint

At the beginning of the 1958 school year, spirits were high in Flint about the future of community schools. The *Flint School Review*, a publication from the Flint Board of Education, ran an article in October 1958 titled "Flint Kindergartners Look to a Bright Future." The article features a photograph of a Flint kindergarten student—Scott—happily running into Merrill Elementary wearing a suit jacket and bow tie. The text of the article is about the expanded course offerings of the "Mott Program" and how Scott and his parents (who are all white) can enjoy the benefits of Flint Community Schools (FCS) for years to come:

> Scott and his classmates can now look forward to an educational program extending well past their high school graduation; to a democratic involvement in community and school affairs, to expert guidance by well-trained teachers and community leaders; to a school program designed to fit their special needs and talents; to the use of physical facilities of all types to house their recreational and educational activities. In short, Scott and his classmates can look to a future brighter perhaps than that of any similar group of children anywhere in the world. (Flint Board of Education, 1958, p. 1)

Flint students who entered kindergarten in 2020 had an incredibly different experience than Scott and his family. For one, most of these students don't look like Scott. As of this writing, students of color in FCS make up 80% of the population, and 83% of students are economically disadvantaged. Students also couldn't walk in the door of a school building in 2020. The COVID-19 pandemic required that FCS start both the 2020–2021 and the 2021–2022 school years "virtually," potentially exacerbating academic challenges already prevalent in the district. As of this writing, less than 10% of students across all grade levels scored at proficient in math in state testing, and less than 12% scored proficient in reading. The high school graduation rate in Flint is only 33% (*U.S. News and World Report*, 2022). Also, unlike Scott, kindergartners who entered school in 2020 were exposed to lead in utero, as their mothers unknowingly drank lead-poisoned water while pregnant with their children in 2014–2015.

What kind of future exists for them?

COMMUNITY SCHOOLS TODAY

Flint remained committed to the community schools model after the Mott Foundation pulled funding. However, as the city experienced more economic challenges after General Motors (GM) left Flint, the goals of community education became harder to fulfill:

> The Flint Community Education Program was asked to become a better program with less money, less staff, and a more challenging clientele. It has been given the responsibility for meeting the needs of a community that is experiencing problems that seem almost insurmountable. (Rohrer & Cady, 1992, p.108)

Community education, even dating back to the days of Frank Manley, had always been "separate" from educational experiences in schools, choosing to focus on after school programming, physical fitness, and adult education. The Mott Foundation had always run its programs through the Flint Board of Education (as was the desire of C. S. Mott), but when they were no longer funding programming, the board of education had to reckon with how to focus on integrating K–12 education and community education when they had not been integrated previously. Also, the Mott Programs were not designed to support integrated schools necessarily, so the coded racial language of "challenging clientele" really meant that the Flint Board of Education was ill-equipped to meet the changing needs of the community, something essential to any community education program (Decker, 1992).

In 2014, the Crim Fitness Foundation stepped in to manage "community education" in Flint. The Crim Fitness Foundation began as an organization to manage the Bobby Crim 10 Mile Road Race, a Flint tradition since 1977. Bobby Crim was an athlete and politician representing Flint in the Michigan House of Representatives. The foundation that started with this race event has since expanded to become a nonprofit dedicated to physical and mental wellness of the city. The Flint Comprehensive Master Plan featured a large role from the Crim Foundation in supporting the overall wellness of the city, which by 2014 included community education. The Crim started by bringing back the role of the Community School Director—a person stationed at each public school in Flint (charter schools as well) to coordinate resources, school and neighborhood programming, and social services. The Crim Foundation handed over community schools programming to the Flint Center for Educational Excellence, founded in 2023 with funding from the C. S. Mott Foundation. However, this still positions community education as outside of K–12 education—an "add-on" as opposed to an integrated element.

Recent research suggests that community schools can be a "place-based school improvement strategy" (Oakes et al., 2017, p. 1) that can improve student achievement in academics while improving the health and wellness of a community (Trujillo et al., 2014). However, recent research also suggests that the quality of community education makes a difference, stressing that community trust is important (Sanders, 2016; Trujillo et al., 2014), as is a "synergy" of classroom instruction and community partnerships (Oakes et al., 2017, p. 6). Since the Crim Foundation took over right as the water crisis was emerging and well before the COVID-19 pandemic began, did they take on more than they bargained for? Are Flint's problems truly insurmountable? If they were described as such in 1992 (Rohrer & Cady, 1992), the argument can certainly be made that things today are not much better. Or perhaps community schools are exactly what Flint needs now, more than ever.

The theme of this chapter is uncertainty. The COVID-19 pandemic lasted more than 2 years and remains a concern for many, though waning overall. Many residents in Flint don't have clean water quite yet, or don't trust it. It remains to be seen how a renewed focus on community schooling in Flint can help improve education, and it may take generations before we see how the water crisis has truly impacted education in the city. This chapter was originally outlined much differently than I had intended when I began this book, as education issues in Flint are continuously evolving. As a result, I am structuring this chapter based on a policy brief from the Learning Policy Institute that reviewed literature on community schools across the country. The authors identified four pillars that appear in most community schools regardless of the logistics on how they operate: (1) integrated student supports, (2) expanded time and learning opportunities, (3) family and community engagement, and (4) collaborative leadership and practices. In this chapter, I look at what FCS and the Crim Foundation have done up to 2023 and hold this up to these pillars to assess how far they've come and how far they have yet to go.

INTEGRATED STUDENT SUPPORTS

In a policy brief, the Learning Policy Institute describe what they reviewed in the literature regarding integrated student supports. They define integrated student supports as those that "address out-of-school barriers to learning through partnerships with social and health services providers" (Oakes et al., 2017, p. 7). They write that, when successful, these supports attend to the "academic, social, emotional, physical, psychological, and moral" development of students in a climate of "safe and trusting relationships" (Oakes et al., 2017, p. 7). Certainly, there was no greater urgency to attend to the education of the whole child and the community once the water crisis became known.

Support for Clean Water

Shamarion Grace is principal at Pierce Elementary School in the East Village Neighborhood of Flint. In 2016, Dr. Grace worked in the central office of FCS and was part of a team that regularly met with the superintendent at the time, Bilal Tawaab. When I asked Dr. Grace what it was like to be in the inner circle of leadership during the time when the world discovered Flint and the injustice there, I expected her to speak of media attention, water bottle donations, and angry and concerned parents. What she told me was that FCS was focused on one thing—getting clean water to the schools. In a crisis so overwhelming and with so much uncertainty, central office focused on one thing they could do something about and made this their top priority.

The school district at first had to manage the intense amount of water bottle donations they were receiving from all over the world and get them to the schools and families who needed them. This is something my student teachers saw at Freeman—cases of water bottles would go home with families regularly so they wouldn't have to wait in line at water distribution sites in the city. But getting the clean water to the school water fountains would prove to be a much bigger task and require the intervention of a Flint outsider—none other than controversial billionaire Elon Musk.

In 2018, Elon Musk donated $480,000 for water filtration systems to be installed in Flint schools (Goetz, 2022a). The school district sought contractors for the installation, including some that had to be monitored through the district's Wi-Fi, or that used LED lights to disinfect the water. This complicated process took 4 years before filters were installed in schools, finally finishing in February 2022 (Goetz, 2022a). And even with filters, students and families must trust the water filtration, which is no simple task. The "safe and trusting relationships" did not exist between Flint residents and any governmental institution—even schools—and may not ever fully recover.

Many FCS students have never known drinking fountains in their schools that were functional or safe. Jacquie Richardson recalled taking her 1st-graders on a trip to the zoo where the children were more fascinated by the working drinking fountains than the animals. However, Dr. Grace has seen glimmers of trust regained in young people. Having been away from in-person schooling for a while now, the students who are returning to Pierce Elementary are more willing to drink from the Elon Musk–funded filtered water fountains there. This is a small step toward regaining trust.

Special Education

At the onset of the water crisis, "integrated student supports" meant providing for students' basic needs for clean water. As the months went on, there became another urgent need to address students' academic and social needs related to lead poisoning. Lead can permanently damage the brain, leading to cognitive delays that can impact academic skills and delays and damage to a child's "executive functioning," which is the part of the brain that regulates behavior. Almost immediately, Jacquie began to see evidence of lead poisoning in her students at Freeman. She noticed her students' attention spans decreasing and an increase in students medicated for ADHD. She noticed her students seemed not to remember concepts she had taught just an hour earlier, which she believes was related to the water crisis. These students need extra support in the form of some kind of special education—or do they?

In Michigan, on average, a school has 12% of students that need an Individual Education Plan (IEP) and special education supports. Prior to the water crisis, 13% of students in Flint received support services (Mitchell, 2019). There were estimations that by 2020, this had risen to 28%. In her study from 2020, Dr. Mona Hanna-Attisha gave cognitive assessments to 172 Flint children and found that 80% of that participant pool would need some form of support for language learning or other intellectual disabilities (Stebbins, 2020). The numbers are not definitive because undoubtably many students have yet to be identified or did not qualify for special education services, despite experiencing academic and behavioral delays.

Other evidence indicates that FCS is unprepared to serve the influx of students needing special education services. In 2016, parents sued FCS and the Genesee Intermediate School District (GISD) for failing to identify students with disabilities, for not following IEP requirements, and for disciplining students with expulsions and suspensions for behavior issues caused by disabilities (Nesbitt, 2020). This failure to meet student needs was exacerbated by a nationwide teacher shortage, where special education teachers were particularly hard to find. Before COVID, 25% of special education teaching positions went unfilled (Nesbitt, 2020)—the pandemic and the "Great Resignation" made things worse.

There is no substitute for high-quality teachers trained specifically to meet the needs of special education students. However, when FCS is in short supply, and with so many students needing support, special education may not be the answer. Dr. Mona posed that we should assume that every child in Flint has been impacted by lead poisoning and respond accordingly (Hanna-Attisha, 2018). Perhaps this means FCS should focus on helping general education teachers adjust their instruction for everyone to include speech and language support, occupational therapy, and autism supports. At the school level, this could include a focus on restorative discipline as opposed to suspensions. Of course, this is asking more of general education teachers, and possibly a moving target as educators are only beginning to learn more about the long-term consequences of the water crisis.

EXTENDED LEARNING TIME AND OPPORTUNITIES

Part of Frank Manley's vision of community schools was that the schools would be open all the time, expanding students' learning time and keeping them out of trouble. Therefore, the FCS model focused so much on afterschool, weekend, and summer classes—the idea is that the learning didn't stop after the school day, week, or year. Now, FCS has tried other approaches to expand learning time.

The school district has tried to increase learning time by adopting a "balanced school calendar." A balanced calendar is not unique to community schools or to Flint; it is a structure to a school year that eliminates a long summer break, where students tend to experience a "summer learning loss" due to being out of school for so long. Instead, students attend school for 45 days at a time followed by a weeklong break called "intercession." In an intercession, students may continue to attend school for enrichment opportunities. In 2016, as a trial run, Freeman Elementary agreed to be the first school to adopt a balanced calendar. By 2019, the entire district had moved to a balanced calendar, with the school year beginning on August 7 that year (Keefer, 2019). However, evidence also suggested that FCS was not prepared to implement a balanced calendar. With a school year beginning in early August in Michigan, it is essential that schools have access to air-conditioning and clean water for children to drink—many Flint school buildings had neither. Temperatures in classrooms in August 2021 reached upward of 100 degrees, which caused the district to close because of excessive heat (Pierret, 2021). Without the proper infrastructure, extended time for learning doesn't make much difference.

And of course, extending time in school became difficult for everyone when the COVID-19 pandemic hit. Like schools across the world, FCS moved to virtual instruction in early 2020. However, unlike other schools, FCS continued virtual schooling well into 2022—nearly 2 years after other area schools had returned to face-to-face instruction. Again, infrastructure issues were cited as the reason—school buildings had poor ventilation, and the teacher shortage meant that substitute teachers were in short supply if staff had to quarantine. COVID-19 hit harder in urban environments, and Flint was no exception. Without clean water, the virus spread faster. In early 2022, the transmission rate in Flint was nearly 40% (Broaddus, 2022). The current superintendent, Kevelin Jones, told CNN he had no regrets keeping children home, citing a better attendance rate in virtual schooling than in face-to-face instruction. However, parents saw virtual schooling as a burden—many parents lost jobs or missed work to stay home to ensure their children kept up with school (Broaddus, 2022). Extending learning time requires not only a commitment to infrastructure at the district level but a societal commitment to the infrastructure of childcare.

FAMILY AND COMMUNITY ENGAGEMENT

A strong community schools model emphasizes strong ties among schools, the community, and families and a "climate of safety and trusting relationships" (Oakes et al., 2017, p. 7). It's not only essential that students have an environment that attends to their social-emotional needs but that their parents do as well. The Flint water crisis has eroded trust in public officials in general. The Crim Fitness Foundation was a good partner to help with this, as their mission for the city includes a focus on improving mental health as much as physical health. And the Crim Foundation brought back the position of the Community School Director to oversee initiatives and rebuild trust within the school buildings.

The idea of a Community School Director (CSD) came from Frank Manley, who had a plan for a community liaison to be at every school to support the connection to the Mott programming. Flint became a training center for CSDs across the country, and Michigan universities began developing graduate programs focused on preparing CSDs in the 1960s (Decker, 1999). Oakes et al. (2017) describe that a good CSD organizes the "synergy" among the school, the students, and the community. When the Mott Foundation pulled funding for the community schools programming in Flint, the role of the CSD disappeared. When the Crim Foundation picked up the ball, the position returned—but is it the same as Manley's vision?

Current CSDs have similar job descriptions to Manley's original vision. Some schools, such as Freeman Elementary, open on weekends for GED courses and skills training for community members. CSDs work with families and get to know students in their buildings. In contrast to Manley's vision, some CSDs are seen as school administrators—almost like an assistant principal—but many do not have school administration backgrounds or experience. Some CSDs follow through on attendance issues in a school, coordinate with school security officers, and manage school volunteers. It could be that the Crim Foundation attempted to more closely integrate "community schooling" with the day-to-day operations of a school, something Manley could never quite manage.

Despite the lack of trust in the school system or in community leaders, evidence shows that families feel attached to their neighborhood schools and want them to succeed. Pierce Elementary, where Dr. Grace is the principal, is a great example of this. Pierce Elementary is in the Flint Cultural Center neighborhood, or the "East Village" neighborhood. As Dr. Grace said, back in the day, Pierce was "*the* school" to attend due to its proximity to the museums and performing arts center, but declining enrollment across the city has put Pierce Elementary in danger of closing. Pierce is a small school, enrolling a total of 141 students in 2022 in grades Pre-K–6. Because of its small size, Dr. Grace believes it's an easy target for the school district to consider closing; however, she says the community schools concept has kept it open. "The small neighborhood school used to be the centerpiece of the neighborhood. At Pierce we're able to do that—the families are close to the school."

A discussion of closing Pierce Elementary was on the agenda of the FCS Board meeting in May 2022. Parents, neighborhood residents, students (current and former), and other administrators attended in protest of a possible closure. According to Dr. Grace, the attachment the neighborhood feels toward their neighborhood school is a remnant of community schooling. FCS has closed several buildings over the last 20 years as the city has downsized in population and in school enrollment. When I worked with the South Parks neighborhood in 2015, before the water crisis, the neighborhood association was lamenting the closure of Stewart Elementary in 2010 and the restructuring of the nearby Brennan Community Center to be for seniors only. Residents told my students during their place-based project in my class that semester that they were concerned about the youth in the neighborhood not feeling connected to that neighborhood because they no longer went to school there. That kind of connection to Pierce is what saved the school from closure. For now.

Closing Flint schools in the 2000s was as much racially motivated as opening schools was in the 1930s. Since 2003, FCS has closed over 20 schools, over half of which have been in predominantly Black neighborhoods (Adams, 2013). Most recently, when discussing whether to close Pierce, the FCS Board cited "structural issues," a common refrain that refers to the physical conditions of the schools and the lack of money to remodel them. However, arguing that schools in Black neighborhoods are older and in worse shape, which is why they need to close, is ignoring the spatial injustices of why these Black neighborhoods have older, dilapidated buildings to begin with. Dr. Grace has frequently mentioned to me and to the media (Goetz, 2022c) that the small number of students at Pierce allows for a better educational experience—and that Pierce students outperform other Flint schools in achievement testing.

If FCS wants to build the trust and connections between schools and the community, closing schools will not help. For CSDs to be successful in revitalizing Manley's vision, it's going to require collaborative leadership, something that FCS lacks.

COLLABORATIVE LEADERSHIP AND PRACTICES

The concept of "collaborative leadership" as a school improvement strategy sometimes refers to the decision-making collaboration at a school level—such as a good relationship between a school principal and the teaching staff. Certainly, collaborative leadership would also include families and parents. According to Oakes and colleagues (2017), collaborative leadership also refers to a "partnerships with community organizations, and district-level cooperative goal setting" (p. 15). Perhaps nothing is on shakier ground in Flint than the tumultuous relationships among the FCS Board of Education, their many superintendents, and community institutions like the Mott and Crim foundations.

It was C. S. Mott's intention that his foundation funding for community schools programming would be managed by the FCS Board of Education. As mentioned in the previous chapter and in Highsmith's work (2015), the Mott Foundation pulled funding for community schools programming in the late 1970s and early 1980s, possibly to avoid complying with the tide of desegregation efforts in the city. Although the Mott Foundation remains tied to initiatives in FCS today, the relationship between the board of education and the foundation still shows cracks from old wounds. For example, the Mott Foundation funded YouthQuest, a city-wide afterschool program that operates in all the FCS schools as well as many of the city's charter schools. This program is the closest thing to the Mott programs of the past, and many families in Flint rely on YouthQuest for afterschool childcare, for tutoring and homework help for their children, and to give their children experiences in the Flint community. YouthQuest was funded by a partnership with many community entities, including FCS and the Crim Foundation. However, the Mott Foundation was its biggest benefactor. In 2021, over a dispute with FCS about transparency in memorandums, the Mott Foundation unexpectedly pulled the funding for YouthQuest in Flint schools, mere weeks before the start of the 2021 school year. Three days later, after a community uproar, the Mott Foundation relented and changed course (Goetz, 2021).

The YouthQuest dispute is one example of the fractured instability between the board of education and the community of Flint. Perhaps the biggest cause of instability is the continuous change in superintendent leadership within the district, seemingly at the whim of the board of education. Since I began my job in Flint in 2013, the district has had six superintendents in those 9 years. Three of those six superintendents ran the district only since I started writing this book in 2020. There may be more by the time this book is published, as only one superintendent since 2005 has served more than 3 years. Leadership turnover of this magnitude is tough for any district, but in a community schools model, district leadership must be closely connected with other community leaders and partners to be effective (Richardson, 2009; Sanders, 2016). Dr. Grace said that with each superintendent, it's like "starting over each time" as the new leader undoes what the previous one did and starts new initiatives, only to have those abandoned when the new person starts. It's hard to build community capital when each leader has only a few months and spends that time arguing with the board of education.

Bilal Tawaab was the superintendent when the water crisis hit, which instantly became his top priority as opposed to other visions he may have had for running the district. Nonetheless, the board rated him ineffective and fired him in 2018. Derrick Lopez was hired in 2018 and then, for reasons unknown, was given an immediate written reprimand and paid suspension a few months later. Educators in Flint I spoke with believed that the board just didn't like Lopez, and didn't like that he wasn't from Flint. It was no surprise that Lopez was fired in 2020. Anita Steward, the former principal of Freeman Elementary with whom I worked closely in 2016, was named superintendent after Lopez. However, Steward made enemies with the board of education when she met with the Mott Foundation about funding for the district without the board's knowledge. The Mott Foundation listed the dispute about who was "allowed" to talk to the foundation from the district as the reason for pulling funding for YouthQuest. Anita Steward resigned after less than a year. As of this writing, Kevelin Jones, who served as an assistant superintendent under Lopez and Stewart, is the superintendent of FCS.

A revolving door of superintendents is the antithesis of a stable school system. But the board itself is not above frequent in-fighting and disagreements, some of which turn physical. In March 2022, Board President Danielle Green physically assaulted another board member during a public meeting (Goetz, 2022b). She resigned her position as part of a plea deal over misdemeanor assault charges (Goetz, 2022d). In another 2022 public meeting, the newly elected board president and vice-president frequently argued and participated in name-calling over issues of transparency (Ford, 2022). The board is the centerpiece of many legal battles in addition to Danielle Green's assault charge. As of this writing, the board of education is being sued for improper dismissal by former superintendents Lopez and Stewart and by a law firm that worked with the district. As mentioned above, the board is also involved in an ACLU lawsuit over not properly providing special education services for students (Ford, 2022).

Collaborative leadership in FCS is nonexistent at the highest levels. This has roots in the board's history with the Mott Foundation and with the spatial injustices of running a school system with little to no resources. However, for the children of Flint, more must be done. The adults must do better.

LEARNING FROM FLINT: PLACE-BASED SCHOOL IMPROVEMENT

I have never been, nor do I ever desire to be, a school or district administrator. I will never claim to be an expert on school improvement from that perspective. However, I do believe that school improvement starts at the classroom level, with teachers. Most of what is mentioned in this chapter involves issues that are well above a teacher's pay grade, but of course it is the teachers who work on the ground with students and therefore are forced to work within these systems. It is important for teachers to understand the context they're in, which includes knowledge of a community's past, present, and possible future.

Taking a critical place inquiry approach to understanding one's community can be a way to fully realize the distribution of resources (or lack of resources) that impact a teacher's ability to engage their students. The process of discovering the "realities" of a community is sometimes called "ground-truthing" (Vélez & Solórzano, 2017). Ground-truthing is an investigation into an entire system such as a school district, a neighborhood, or how the systems work together to uncover what spatial inequities may exist there, or what assets may be available. Importantly, ground-truthing doesn't only include looking at statistics or quantitative data but involves studying the lived experiences of community members, examinations of the physical environment, and even an exploration into history (Carp, 2008). For this chapter, I used quite a few secondary sources (historical and current) and reported demographic data, as well as interviews with community members and school administrators, to "ground-truth" this chapter in the real outcomes of the Flint water crisis. Here are some other ways teachers can ground-truth their communities to serve their students in the name of "school improvement" as well as to meet social studies standards:

- Students can take part in "ground-truthing" their communities as a precursor to taking informed action. Have students "ground-truth" data on a community need and partner with an organization that meets this need. For example, in Flint, the local food bank addresses the need for food security in the city. Have students research what food security is, why food insecurity is a problem, and how to address it.
- Have students collaborate with their families on social studies tasks and assessments. Some possibilities are community historical research, a family memoir, or a service project. Families are integral parts of community schools (Keith, 1996) and can be the students' first touchpoint with place-based education right at home.
- To develop your own learning about the place you teach in as well as to build strong family and community connections, branch out

of the classroom. Organize and/or attend family nights at school to meet parents and caregivers. If appropriate, make invited and scheduled home visits to your students' families to better understand the context they're living in.
- Since teachers must work in the realities of systems (functioning or not), teachers should take informed action themselves when it comes to shaping these systems. Attend school board meetings to understand the distribution of resources in your school district. Pay close attention to school board candidates around election time. Don't be afraid to ask them questions about integrated student supports, connections to families and community resources, and their approach to collaborative leadership.

At the beginning of this chapter, I asked what kind of future remains for the kindergartners of the 2020s—the ones who don't look like Scott from 1958, the ones who started school in a pandemic and who have urgent learning support needs after overexposure to lead. In Flint, the answer remains uncertain. Families still distrust authority, and a constant rotation of superintendents and an unstable board of education does not help. There is a considerable lack of capital (monetary and human capital) to provide special education services to the number of students in Flint who may need them. And a looming threat remains that a neighborhood school may be closed, and with it the closure of a chapter of the community schools model. Yet, despite threats of her school closing year after year, Dr. Grace is one school administrator who retains hope: "There is some hope for us to get on the right track. I would love to see that before I retire. If we have the supports, we can get [the students] through this."

Part II

HOW CAN SCHOOLING BE REIMAGINED TO CENTER "PLACE"?

CHAPTER 4

Designing Early Childhood Education in Flint

When my daughter Maggie was 5 months old in the late summer of 2015, I had to return to work in Flint. Maggie was enrolled in the Early Childhood Development Center (ECDC) infant room on the University of Michigan-Flint campus since before she was born, and luckily she was out of the hospital and healthy enough to keep our plans. At that time, the ECDC had web cameras in the rooms so parents could log in with a password and watch their child at times throughout the day. Like a typical new mom, I dropped my first child off at her first day of childcare and then proceeded to watch the webcam the entire day rather than work. Right about the time when I was regretting my choice to go back to work (after all, watching my kid all day without doing work defeats the purpose of childcare!), I saw Ms. Carolyn, Maggie's infant room teacher, bring out a box of musical instruments. She and the other teachers sat in a circle with infants on their laps and handed the children different instruments. Although the webcam had no sound, I could "hear" the classroom as each of the infants shook different instruments and banged them on surfaces (the floor, the teacher's knees, etc.) to see what would happen.

It was at this moment that I realized Maggie was getting a different kind of experience at the ECDC than I could provide her at home. Maggie lost oxygen at some point during her birth, which resulted in a permanent traumatic brain injury called hypoxic ischemic encephalopathy (HIE). Extremely rare in full-term babies like Maggie (less than 2% of full-term babies have any form), HIE can lead to developmental delays, cognitive impairments, and other physical ailments such as hearing and vision loss. Maggie was diagnosed as having a "moderate" case of HIE, which means it was likely she would experience some of those conditions, but the degree to which she would suffer from them could vary widely. Whereas some doctors weren't optimistic, a nurse practitioner named Janet took a different approach. She reminded me that the brain is plastic and moldable, especially with children. She said that with good nutrition and a strong education with proper supports, Maggie's brain could "remap" itself and minimize negative outcomes from the HIE. When I saw Ms. Carolyn bring out the musical instruments and let Maggie play with them while allowing her to look at the faces of others around her, I realized the ECDC was going to be an important partner in Maggie's brain development.

The educator in me was also recognizing that Ms. Carolyn was providing an inquiry-based environment for Maggie to explore what she found curious. Later that afternoon, Carolyn texted me a picture of Maggie outside in a stroller, holding and staring intently at a flower Carolyn had picked for her from the campus grounds during a walk. Although Carolyn's text was meant to ease a new mom's worries (and it did!), the picture also helped me realize how much place-based education in social studies borrows from early childhood educators and scholars. Maggie's brain was working overtime that day as she learned from her environment in the city of Flint, and her moldable brain was literally being formed by that same place.

As the trauma of the water crisis caused many to focus on the moldable yet possibly damaged brains of Flint's children and how to minimize negative consequences of lead poisoning, educators and parents in Flint started asking the question *How can schooling be reimagined?* as a response to the crisis. This question has been asked across the world since the COVID-19 pandemic, as traditional schools were upended by virtual learning and then had to consider what returning to face-to-face learning would look like in the middle of a global pandemic and in an age of reckoning with racial injustices. Many, including scholar Gloria Ladson-Billings, advocated that a return to "normal" wasn't going to be good enough (Ladson-Billings, 2021). Perhaps living through numerous national and global tragedies and traumatic events might be the catalyst to changing how we approach educating our children. In the next few chapters, I use critical place inquiry (Tuck & McKenzie, 2015) to examine the ways that educational entities in the city embraced place-based education as a call to action to respond to the needs of Flint's children. This is a true enactment of community education; as Decker noted in 1992, "community education must be viewed as a process, not as a program. Its major components must continue to change as community conditions change" (p. 10). Early childhood educators in Flint were some of the first to embrace the idea that community conditions had changed, and that they must adapt as well. The question is not just "how can schooling be reimagined," but "how can schooling be reimagined to center 'place?'"

EARLY CHILDHOOD EDUCATION AND LEAD POISONING

According to the 2020 census, there are roughly 6,000 children under the age of 5 living in Flint; 64% of them identify as Black, Hispanic, or more than one race. The median household income in Flint is $30,383 annually. For comparison, the median income in the nearby suburb of Grand Blanc is more than double this number (United States Census Bureau, n.d.b). It's perhaps easy to see the water crisis as something Flint children must face *in addition to* poverty and racism, however, that masks the fact that Flint children are facing the impact of lead poisoning *because of* their race and income levels (Blaisdell, 2017). The connectivity of these factors must be understood before meaningful action can be taken.

Early in the water crisis, it was essential that educators and parents understood what lead poisoning is, how it affects children, and what can be done to minimize negative outcomes. Medical studies on lead poisoning have been done for a long time, as the prevalence of lead in everyday household items used to be much greater. Lead-based paint in older houses is the main cause of lead poisoning in children today, as sometimes kids ingest lead-based paint chips while crawling around or exploring in their homes. No amount of lead is acceptable to ingest for anyone—children or adults—and in 1991, the Environmental Protection Agency (EPA) published a regulation called the Lead & Copper Rule (LCR) to prevent lead from being ingested in a water supply. The LCR requires certain lead testing protocols for water pipes through testing a sample of buildings across a water utility service area and other protocols for what to do if the lead levels exceed the 15 parts per billion (ppb) action level, including notifying residents and replacing lead service lines. In Flint, the regional EPA's enforcement of the LCR was haphazard at best, even as residents complained about something being wrong with their water after the switch to the Flint River source. Testing protocols were not followed, causing lead levels to report as lower than they really were, which meant that reporting and replacing protocols were not happening either. Even with poor testing procedures, the lead in LeeAnn Walters's home tested at *400* ppb (Hanna-Attisha, 2018, p. 56).

Lead poisoning from paint or water is incredibly harmful to children. Lead enters the bloodstream and then settles in tissue, bones, and the brain. There, it takes up space meant for nutrients like calcium. Lead destroys gray matter in the brain, causing developmental delays, loss of cognitive ability, and loss of executive functioning, which can result in uncontrollable aggression or attention issues (Hanna-Attisha, 2018). Despite the damage that's possible, the LCR didn't apply to lead testing in schools and childcare facilities until 2022, and even then, it was partially as a response to the Flint water crisis (Schirra, 2022). As a direct response to what we learned from the water crisis, Michigan now has the strictest LCRs in the country, requiring that all lead pipes in the state be replaced by 2035, and that health emergencies be issued when lead over 12 ppb is detected in a water supply (MI Lead Safe, 2023). Changing policies around lead testing is just one way Michigan and the rest of the country has learned from the Flint water crisis. Children's moldable brains means there are ways that the results of lead poisoning can be minimized through what Dr. Mona calls an "ecobiodevelopmental approach" (Hanna-Attisha, 2018, p. 271) that attacks the different levels of spatial injustices Flint kids experience and provide interventions to entire systems—nutrition, transportation, childcare, physical and mental health services, and much more.

An ecobiodevelopmental approach recognizes that the numerous oppressive systems in Flint compound and exacerbate one another. For example, a healthy, nutritious diet is important to combating the effects of lead poisoning. However, nearly half of Flint's population in 2019 lived more than a mile away from a supermarket, and the primarily Black neighborhoods in Flint had the least access to healthy and affordable food options, rendering Flint a "food desert." For many, liquor stores and convenience stores are sources of food because they accept food stamps (Ahmad, 2019). Intervention is needed to break this cycle. One source of healthy food in the city of Flint is the Flint Farmers' Market. With a donation from billionaire Tom Gores (a Flint native), every family attending a Flint school or early childhood center was given gift certificates to the Farmers' Market to purchase fresh food. In 2016, Gores's donations also enabled schools to give out food to families over weekends and school breaks. Freeman Elementary gave backpacks full of food to their students' families.

Research suggests that access to high-quality preschool and early childhood education can benefit families and children for generations. Economist James Heckman studied Black children in Ypsilanti, Michigan, who attended preschool in 1967 and then followed up with 85% of the original participants well into adulthood in 2019. When compared to nonparticipants in the study, as adults, these children were more likely to complete high school without suspension, more likely to be fully employed, less likely to have been arrested, and more likely to be physically healthier (Heckman & Karapakula, 2019). These findings are some of the first to employ an experimental design to show the positive impact of early childhood education on overall health outcomes for children in poverty.

In 2014, 34% of 3- and 4-year-olds in Flint attended preschool, according to the Greater Flint Health Coalition (GFHC & PPHI, 2023). Once the water crisis hit, there was immediate intervention from public entities to increase access to early childhood education for Flint families. The Michigan Department of Health and Human Services (DHHS) allowed any child born in a certain window during the switch to Flint River water to attend a licensed childcare facility for free or at an extremely reduced cost. These are benefits typically given to the state's Great Start Readiness Program (GSRP), a preschool that is free for low-income families statewide. However, this new DHHS program allowed any child, regardless of income, to attend a preschool or childcare center up to the age of 4. The Genesee Intermediate School District (GISD) provided occupational therapists and speech/language pathologists to Great Start Readiness Preschools in Flint free of charge for the school and parents, one example of universally allowing all children access to these services regardless of whether they were exposed to lead.

Starletta Rett-Henry and Marissa Cobleigh are two of my former UM-Flint students, who after graduation worked extensively in early childhood settings in Flint, helping early childhood centers, teachers, and parents mitigate the effects of lead poisoning on Flint's kids. Marissa worked as an Early Childhood Specialist Assistant for the GISD, a job that existed because of state grants and a collaboration with Flint Community Schools (FCS). She traveled to different early childhood centers in Flint, mostly those that were within FCS. She worked with teachers, coaching them on how to address behavior exhibited by children with a lack of executive functioning from lead poisoning and how to create an inclusive classroom. Once Marissa noticed that support systems like speech teachers and autism specialists were becoming less frequently available, she coached teachers on how to give their students speech interventions in their general classrooms. After about 5 years of her work, money from the state and from FCS began to run dry, as public entities began to determine that the water crisis was "over" and no longer needed monetary support. Marissa then began to help parents become advocates for their children as they fought for special education services in their elementary schools.

Starletta had been working in early childhood centers and elementary schools in Flint since well before the pandemic. She had returned to UM-Flint to get her official elementary teaching certificate, and had also completed her student teaching at Freeman Elementary, a semester after Hana did in the fall of 2016. In her kindergarten classroom there, she was seeing cognitive delays from her students after what was now more than a year of lead exposure. However, she described the academic interventions as "same old, same old" and mentioned that poor attendance didn't help. In her experience, the lack of equitable supports for Flint children once they're in early childhood settings is what she considers the biggest problem facing education in the city today. Nonetheless, she said her experience at Freeman taught her the importance of focusing on the social-emotional aspect of learning for the children, and even the parents, above all else. As she entered a position as a Young Fives teacher in nearby Grand Blanc, she said her ability to connect with parents, children, and families' social-emotional needs helped her tremendously during the pandemic, as did her ability to "pivot"—a popular buzzword in COVID-era education.

Despite the challenges of providing quality supports to Flint children, there is still evidence that some supports were working, particularly the DHHS childcare tuition credit. By 2020, the percentage of 3- and 4-year-olds in Flint attending preschool had risen to 51%, a nearly 50% increase from 2014, and above the state of Michigan average (GFHC & PPHI, 2023). The Heckman and Karapakula (2019) study has shown that this access alone can have a positive effect on Flint families for generations—certainly a move in the right direction. In an interview about his landmark study, Heckman was clear in saying that he hopes his research offers evidence of the importance of social-emotional learning in these early childhood education programs, even more so than cognitive outcomes. Heckman hopes that instead of his study being used to advocate for "universal preschool" that it should push policymakers to design interventions for certain populations based on need—in other words, a place-based approach to childcare systems (Wang, 2019). In the next part of this chapter, I show how two groups in Flint did exactly what Heckman advocated for—designing tailored early childhood systems in the city grounded in the community needs.

CHILDCARE IN FORMAL SETTINGS

Jodi Ramos chuckled at me when I asked her how she got her start in early childhood education. She said she never wanted to be a teacher—her mother was a teacher in FCS and later a principal, and she had seen how much work it was. She was a theater major with intentions to work as an artist. During college at Michigan State University, she added an education major to her theater major just to have something to fall back on and "pay the bills"—but even then, she was focused on secondary education. After graduation, she subbed in a Head Start classroom with 3- and 4-year-old students and fell in love with the program's focus on family and community involvement. Having grown up in Flint, with her mother in education, she witnessed firsthand how important the neighborhood "community" school was to families. "Your school is your family. It helped raise you." Subbing in Head Start made her realize that a career in early childhood education checked off her desire to work in a profession where she could give back to the community of Flint. Jodi went back to school at Mott Community College in Flint to get her associate degree in Early Childhood Education and was working as a Head Start teacher when the water crisis hit.

Federally funded early childhood programs such as Head Start (ages 3–5) and Early Head Start (ages 0–3) and state-funded early childhood programs like GSRP in Michigan have been operating in Flint for a long time in various locations around the city—some at elementary schools in FCS, others at private early childhood centers, like the ECDC on UM-Flint's campus. These programs have always been free for families that meet the income eligibility requirements. Once the water crisis hit, it became clear that a significant investment in gaining children access to quality early childhood education was essential to their development. The Mott Foundation was ready to step in. In partnership with the GISD, the Community Foundation of Greater Flint, and FCS, the Mott Foundation helped to open Educare Flint—an early childhood center that was the first of its kind in Michigan.

Educare is a model of early childhood education in the country, originally out of Chicago. There are many Educare schools around the country, each separately managed. However, every Educare school follows the model of four "core features": (1) high-quality teaching practices—hiring trained early childhood teachers and using research-based practices; (2) data utilization—making data-driven decisions about teaching and learning; (3) embedded professional development—coaching early childhood teachers in their classrooms; and (4) intensive family and community engagement with smaller caseloads than a typical Head Start program (Educare, n.d.). Educare schools serve children ages 0–5, but are in session year-round, 5 days a week. Most Head Start programs are not that comprehensive, usually closing in the summers, following a public-school calendar. GSRP runs only during the school year and for only 4 days a week. Bringing Educare to Flint would give families another option for high-quality early childhood education that is more accessible and, with the funding of the Mott Foundation, free.

Educare Flint opened in December 2017 with 200 students from infants to preschoolers in 18 classrooms, using part of one of Flint's largest elementary school campuses—Durant-Tuuri-Mott Elementary (Carmody, 2017). Jodi Ramos was the school's inaugural School Coordinator, a role similar to school principal. Jodi started her career as an early childhood educator looking to build community, and Educare offered her an opportunity to do just that. She applied for the job because of the Educare model and its commitment to research. Each Educare school must also have a research partner to meet its core value of data utilization, and Jodi was working on her doctorate at the time, finding herself fully immersed in research and eager to apply it in her work at Educare to help Flint families.

According to Jodi, health care was a top priority among parents—not surprising, given the lead exposure and the sicknesses children in Flint had been suffering from as a result. So, Jodi and Ja'Nel Jamerson, Educare Flint's Executive Director, sought community partners in health fields—the Michigan Department of Health and Human Services (MDHHS) and Mott Children's Hospital were early partners, offering lead testing and fluoride treatments for children on site at Educare. Jodi told me that parents needed the convenience of being able to take care of what they needed at school as they were dropping off or picking up their children. The pediatric residency program at Hurley Hospital in Flint brought residents to the school to do observations and basic checkups on children not only to build their knowledge base on the impacts of lead poisoning but also to offer suggestions of services to families based on medical observation and data.

Flint's lack of access to healthy food was also a concern to Educare families. The WIC (Women Infant and Children) program would come to the school to help parents get registered for the program, answer questions, and offer support. With funding from the Mott Foundation, Community Foundation of Greater Flint, FCS, and the GISD (who call themselves the Flint Early Childhood Collective or FECC), Educare Flint runs a "pop-up market" where families can take home large bags of fresh fruits and vegetables a few times a week for free.

And these supports appear to be working. In the fall of 2022, Educare Flint sent its first class of 34 students (who had been with the school since it opened in 2017) to kindergarten. These children came to Educare as infants and stayed with the same two or three teachers throughout their time at the school. Jodi calls the "continuity of care" one of Educare's strengths. Because they spend years with the same children, teachers get to know their individual strengths and challenges quite well and develop tight connections with their families that help to inform what the school could be doing better to meet their needs. Generally, by age 3, children who enter Head Start from "at-risk" environments such as Flint are behind on assessment standards in social and emotional learning and language learning. Jodi says she doesn't see this in Educare Flint's 3-year-olds. They enter their Head Start classrooms more in line with the average. And although possible cognitive delays from lead poisoning are hard to measure at such a young age, Jodi believes Educare Flint sent these 34 children to kindergarten better prepared to learn because they had more opportunities to practice following routines and listening skills—important executive functioning tasks needed for school. These children spread out into Genesee County for kindergarten, but thanks to a data-sharing agreement among members of the FECC, it will be possible to track the long-term progress of all Educare students enrolled in FCS.

Although Educare is a nationwide model, the team at Educare Flint was determined to listen to Flint families to understand how the school could support them as part of the community. This is the community school model that Jodi grew up with—the one that Frank Manley envisioned. However, this time, the families worked with the community school to determine the proper supports they needed and how Educare Flint could help, instead of imposing support on them. Jodi strongly believes in public schooling and the community school model; she believes that neighborhood schools were damaged with school choice options such as waivers, charter schools, and vouchers, but she was quick to remind me that "it's expensive to run early childhood programs, and there isn't as much funding as [K–12] education gets." Because of this, many early childhood centers rely on private funding or other grant funding to sustain community initiatives. So, also comparable to Manley's vision, community schools like Educare Flint needed a private benefactor to become a reality.

USING HUMAN-CENTERED DESIGN TO RESPOND TO EARLY CHILDHOOD NEEDS

Although the number of Flint children in preschool programs has risen since 2014, roughly half of Flint's 3- and 4-year-olds are still being cared for by friends, family members, and neighbors, who are called FFN providers (Oshio & Kupperman, 2021). Sometimes, these FFN providers take care of many children in their home, children who may or may not be related to them. In the United States, a third of children under 5 are taken care of by FFN providers, and for children 2 and younger, FFN providers are the most common type of childcare (Oshio & Kupperman, 2021).

FFN providers are common in areas considered "childcare deserts"—places with little access to licensed childcare programs. These places have a lower median income, large minority populations, or low population density. Flint doesn't exactly qualify as a childcare desert, as there are many licensed programs for families to access, but for convenience parents typically use friends and family for childcare. Childcare centers like Educare are not open in the very early morning, later in the evening, over a third shift, or on weekends. Whether or not children are enrolled in a licensed program should not be the gatekeeper for the benefits that a center like Educare provides.

Dr. Toko Oshio, an associate professor of early childhood education at UM-Flint, was involved early in the research aspects of Educare when it first opened, and she was interested in developing online resources for childcare providers in Flint as a response to the water crisis. Toko teamed up with Dr. Jeff Kupperman, a former educational technology professor at UM-Flint, to help develop her idea. Jeff encouraged Toko to use a human-centered design approach to her project. Human-centered design has been a practice in the fields of technology (Cooley, 2000), business (Landry, 2020), and engineering (Boy, 2013; Zoltowski et al., 2013) and involves designing a product with a "user" in mind—one that serves a purpose or fills a real need that people have, as opposed to a purpose or need the designer *thinks* they need. When Toko was looking to provide resources for childcare providers, Jeff encouraged her to spend more time considering what childcare providers in Flint really needed.

Human-centered design goes hand in hand with place-based education and the concept of ground-truthing (Vélez & Solórzano, 2017, p. 22). Place-based education is a reciprocal relationship between school and a "place" or "community." When educators are looking to get students involved with community partners, the tendency is to come in with a project idea first, or a solution to a perceived problem first. But place-based education is about learning *with* and *from* a community, which means that school systems, individual educators, and students must spend time examining what a community needs by learning from community members themselves. Toko did the same—she spent time learning from Flint residents and childcare providers to discover which resources would be the most helpful to them. When she learned of the prevalence of FFN providers and how they were often missing from the early childhood interventions from the water crisis, she tailored her project to this specific need.

With help from a W. K. Kellogg Foundation grant, Toko and Jeff created the Provider Empowerment Program (PEP). The PEP website is full of resources that FFN providers said they needed: access to food and water distribution; ways to obtain children's clothing, toys, and diapers; and help with navigating health care systems and technology (Provider Empowerment Program, 2020). However, families indicated that receiving resources via text message was their preferred mode of communication. PEP now texts ideas for learning activities, games, and healthy recipes three times a week to over 140 subscribers through their text-messaging service (University of Michigan, 2021). Providing resources via text message was not what Toko had originally envisioned for the project, but it was an example of using human-centered, place-based design in her research; FFN providers preferred to access their information through texting.

Toko recalled a family who wanted a "pack and play" for the toddler granddaughter they took care of. (A "pack and play" is a portable crib where toddlers and infants can sleep or play in a confined space.) She considered the ways she could help this family set up a learning environment in their living room so the toddler need not be confined to a pack and play—her expertise in child development coming out! She recalls how she paused to consider why the family needed the pack and play. For example, sometimes their toddler just needed a confined space so the family could cook dinner or take a phone call without having to have an eye on the child. In a case where Toko believed the lack of access was education about toddler development, the FFN provider believed the lack of access was to a specific resource—a pack and play. Needless to say, Toko found a pack and play for the family.

The lack of access to institutional childcare is a spatial injustice, and certainly in Flint, the lack of availability of water crisis resources for FFN providers is an example of inequities in access. Out of a desire to help others out of the water crisis, Toko found that perhaps what she saw as an injustice or access issue wasn't one at all. Some families prefer FFN providers for their children. Parents tend to trust family members over institutions such as childcare centers, and institutional preschools may not share the same cultural values (Dow, 2016). Instead of telling families to send their children to childcare centers, PEP helps FFN providers to become licensed childcare providers themselves. This is the empowerment piece of the Provider Empowerment Program. Many friends and family members don't consider themselves "childcare providers" because taking care of family is just what families do. And while this is certainly true, licensed home childcare centers receive subsidies on food, diapers, and household supplies that FFN providers miss out on. PEP provides consulting for FFN providers that choose to become licensed, helping them navigate through often complex licensing requirements from the state. Not only does becoming licensed help some FFN providers have access to more services, but in some cases, it's empowering women in Flint to become entrepreneurs, running their own in-home childcare center businesses. The next step for PEP is to tackle policy issues around the barriers to FFN providers gaining access to childcare licensing and subsidies.

LEARNING FROM FLINT: DESIGNING PLACE-BASED EDUCATION

This chapter has highlighted examples of how the Flint community has rallied around early childhood education to minimize the effects of lead poisoning on children in the city. With Educare, it was reinvigorating a community school model targeting specific needs of the community. With PEP, it was through listening to the voices of those who were often missing from the conversations on water crisis interventions—FFN providers. In both examples, water crisis interventions are deeply rooted in place and driven by the community. Here are other ways educators can think about place-based interventions in the classroom and in research:

- Try a human-centered design approach to "community problems." Many state social studies standards, including those in Michigan, advocate for students to work on addressing a public issue. For example, a 1st-grade social studies standard in Michigan is to "Identify public issues in the local community that influence people's daily lives." Have students attend community meetings to get a sense of what really matters to residents.
- Always include community members in any "solutions" to issues that involve them. Ask residents what *they* think solutions to community issues are, and talk together about how your students can help them achieve their goals.

Educating the children of Flint who have been impacted by lead poisoning will require a community effort. The ecobiodevelopmental approach to education that Dr. Mona advocates requires a collaboration from parents, educators, public school systems, childcare centers, the medical field, local businesses, and philanthropic foundations. These interests need to work harmoniously for the good of Flint's children, which is no easy feat. There is a long history of Flint's institutions (e.g., General Motors, state and city governments, FCS) failing their residents, but it is their responsibility to rectify these injustices by listening to what the community requires for solutions.

CHAPTER 5

Reggio-Inspired Education in Flint

A group of 4-year-olds approach First Street in Flint. Their teacher at their Reggio-inspired preschool sings a song about looking both ways before they cross the street. Before they step onto First Street to cross it, one preschooler stops the class. "Ms. Jen—look! The weather ball! It's so close!" The "weather ball" is a famous Flint landmark—in 1956, this white sphere was installed 70 feet above the 10th floor of the First Merit Bank building in downtown Flint, and it has been a part of the Flint skyline ever since, even as the bank has changed owners over the years (now owned by Huntington Bank) (Acosta, 2018). The ball changes colors to predict the weather—a red ball means "warmer ahead," blue means "cold temperatures are due," and a blinking ball means "rain or snow likely" (see Figure 5.1). For almost 70 years, children and adults alike have excitedly looked at the skyline to see what color the weather ball is showing, and Ms. Jen's preschool class was no different.

Jen Cozart teaches preschool at the Early Childhood Development Center (ECDC) on the University of Michigan-Flint's campus. Although it is located on campus, the center is open to anyone in the Flint community. The center is tuition-based, but it does have two Great Start Readiness Preschool

Figure 5.1. *The Famous Flint Weather Ball Showing "Warmer Ahead"*

(GSRP) classrooms subsidized by the state for families. The entire center is "Reggio-inspired"—a constructivist, hands-on approach to early childhood and early elementary age instruction. Jen is taking her class on one of many walks to the Flint Farmers' Market a few blocks from the ECDC. This time, she has given a few students the job of "photographer." Today's photographer snaps a picture of the weather ball before the class joins hands with their friends and teachers to cross First Street where the Farmers' Market is located.

Approaches to early childhood and elementary education grounded in place-based pedagogy like the Reggio philosophy have many connections to social studies inquiry and education for civic engagement. This chapter describes what place-based education looked like for some preschoolers in Flint in the Reggio-inspired ECDC, and how the children at the ECDC presented a counternarrative of Flint that honors the way they see the city.

REGGIO EMILIA AS PLACE-BASED EDUCATION

As mentioned earlier, I sent both of my daughters to UM-Flint's ECDC when they were infants. My oldest, Maggie, stayed at the Reggio-inspired center until kindergarten; my youngest, McKenzie, attended until the COVID lockdowns started. From the minute I looked at the webcam on Maggie's first day, I immediately saw the similarities of the Reggio Emilia philosophy to inquiry instruction, and this changed how I thought about social studies education, place-based education, and my own research.

The Reggio Emilia philosophy of education began in post–World War II Italy when Loris Malaguzzi collaborated with a group of parents to literally reimagine what education could look like in their war-torn town of Reggio Emilia. These parents imagined that their children, born during wartime, would need to be educated in a system that valued citizenship and anti-fascism. To be self-reliant, children should be allowed to pursue their passions while being treated as capable beings. This mirrors what Ladson-Billings (2021) called for post-pandemic: not a return to what was before, but to learn from what came before to reimagine a different type of education for the future.

The Reggio approach values a strong commitment to using the community or the environment as a guide for students' inquiries (Edwards et al., 2012). The parents in Reggio Emilia, Italy, collaborated with Malaguzzi to create a curriculum and learning experiences that addressed the specific needs of the children in their community. Because of this, all centers and schools who use the Reggio philosophy can call themselves "Reggio-inspired" or "Reggio-based," acknowledging that the curriculum can't be replicated the same way in a different place (Jones, 2023).

A Reggio-inspired education is place-based education by design. A tenet of the Reggio Emilia philosophy is that the environment is the "third teacher," right behind educators and families. The Reggio Approach website describes that in a Reggio-inspired classroom, "the environment interacts, modifies, and takes shape in relation to the projects and learning experiences, in a constant dialogue between architecture and pedagogy" (Reggio Emilia Approach, 2022). Although the website defines the environment as both interior and exterior spaces, most of the intention is on the educator's design of a classroom's interior space to meet the needs of the children and to serve their interests, inquiries, and projects.

However, children also interact with the natural, exterior environment. Although Reggio educators can't presume to design the community to meet their students' needs, they certainly can design experiences where students interact with their natural environment. Environmental education is a vast field of study with connections to place-based education. Scholars I cite frequently in social studies also use environmental education as place-based examples, including Amy Demarest (2015) and Gregory Smith (Smith & Sobel, 2010), who focus primarily on environmental education with secondary students because they have fewer opportunities in their school day to spend outdoors. Fikile Nxumalo (2019) writes specifically about environmental education in early childhood, calling attention to how children in early childhood classrooms interact with nature in ways that perpetuate settler colonialism, such as when teachers position nature or "the environment" as existing to be a learning space for children, just waiting to be "discovered" by them.

Whereas the Reggio approach calls the environment the "third teacher," Nxumalo reminds us that the environment (whether rural or urban) has its own stories rooted in Indigenous knowledge, with "more-than-human" presences. She writes of "reconfiguring presences" (2019, p. 52) and calls on scholars to rethink how we approach place-based education to be less focused on the child as the actor and place as the backdrop. For example, creating and tending a community garden is often touted as a place-based pedagogical activity. In Chapter 2, I mentioned how Jacquie Richardson engaged her students in tending a garden and selling vegetables to serve the Flint community. Other studies such as one from Erin Casey and colleagues also highlight how citizenship education appears in a Reggio-inspired preschool through a social studies inquiry on the school's garden (Casey et al., 2019). Nxumalo (2019) points out that arbitrary boundaries of community gardens reinforce settler colonialism by determining what land is worth tending and what land is "wild," not to mention the history of community gardens promoting capitalism and patriotism during World War II.

Indeed, I saw a lot of place-based education at the ECDC that took the learning from the classroom out into the city of Flint, with the city as a backdrop for learning. And one might argue that these place-based, Reggio-inspired practices are reinforcing settler colonialism by treating the city as a learning environment for children, as opposed to a place with its own stories and more-than-human entities (Nxumalo, 2019). However, it is precisely because of Flint's stories of its past with segregation and redlining and its present and future of environmental injustice of the water crisis that it's important for children to be out in the city to develop their own narratives, and to have these honored as well.

BUILDING PLACE-CONSCIOUSNESS IN A REGGIO TODDLER CLASSROOM

In many ways, a toddler classroom is primed for place-based education. After all, babies and toddlers learn from experiences in their environment constantly. They splash in water to see what it feels like, they throw a toy across the room to see what the reaction will be (both the toy's reaction and the reaction of their caregiver), and they are naturally curious about the world around them. Their perspective on their environment influences everything from early literacy, brain development, early mathematical concepts, and social-emotional well-being.

"Place" is one of the five themes of geography (Gersmehl, 2014), and in the field of geography, understanding place means understanding the characteristics of a specific location—what human-made and naturally made features are there? What is the culture there? Who lives there and why? When toddlers and preschoolers can get out into their environment, they can begin to learn the answers to these basic human geography questions. Brillante and Mankiw (2015) suggest taking children on walks around the neighborhood, planning family events in the community, and helping children pay specific attention to their environment by pointing out landmarks. Part of Sobel's concept of "pedagogy of place" (2005, p. 11) is that the community looks to students as valuable resources for change, and the school curriculum gives students space to be agents for change, a natural connection to the concept of taking informed action in social studies (NCSS, 2013).

To prepare students to be agents of change, place-based education with toddlers needs to attend to the ideas of place-consciousness (Gruenewald, 2003a), where students reflect on their personal experiences with a place to understand how to engage in it. Gaining this understanding of their place can lead the children eventually to placemaking (Fettes & Judson, 2011), the process of shaping the places where we belong (Gruenewald, 2003a). Building place-consciousness with toddlers can be relatively easy because their natural curiosity makes them open to new experiences. For 2-year-olds, this reflection happens through intentional experiences and discussions, guided by their teacher.

Sharneese's Campus Walks

My youngest daughter McKenzie attended the ECDC until the COVID lockdowns of 2020. Most of her 3 years at the ECDC, she was taught by Sharneese, one of my former students. Sharneese grew up in Flint, and she was eager to take her students around the city, even though they were so young—ages 1 or 2 years old. She invited me to stay after morning drop-off one day so I could see how she incorporated place-based social studies into her morning meeting. Of course, I could not pass up this opportunity to see Sharneese apply what she had learned in my class while teaching my daughter.

Shortly after the morning meeting began, Sharneese pulled out a stack of pictures. She asked, "Do you all remember the different places we go around the school? Let's see if we remember." She held up the first picture, clearly taken by her or another teacher, of McKinnon Plaza—an area on the UM-Flint campus near my office. McKinnon Plaza is a courtyard with several steps leading up to Kearsley Street in Flint. There is also a long, winding accessibility ramp for those who don't want to use the stairs. "Where is this?" Sharneese asked as she held up the picture.

My daughter immediately jumped out of my lap. "RUN!" she announced.

"Yes, McKenzie! We do run here! This is the ramp in McKinnon Plaza!" Sharneese handed the picture to my daughter to keep, and she clutched it to her chest while Sharneese pulled out several other pictures of campus landmarks for the students to identify. The other 2-year-olds popped up and yelled out seemingly random words that all described these important places on campus ("water!" for the Flint River, "rock!" for a sculpture on campus). This was an example of students reflecting on their experiences in Flint. Using Sharneese's photos as prompts, they were remembering the actions they took in specific spots and the names they gave to these places.

Sharneese frequently takes walks through campus with the toddlers when the weather is warm. It's not unusual to be a UM-Flint student and see a dozen toddlers holding on to a rope, their hands around attached plastic rings, as they excitedly identify all their favorite places and their own names for them, including "Circle Arch" and "Rainbow Rock"—the toddlers' names for sculptures on campus. Taking these walks is an important activity to build the students awareness of place and their geographic knowledge (Brillante & Mankiw, 2015), but getting to the point where the toddlers can take a stroll around campus wasn't simple.

Many teachers at the ECDC take children on walks around the campus or the Flint community, but these trips happen most often with the preschool-age students (ages 4 or 5 or in the infant and early toddler classrooms (ages 0 to 1), where teachers can take children on walks in strollers. Sharneese's children were 2 years old—too big for most strollers, but not quite at the age where they can manage long walks or easily follow safety directions. Taking walks with the 2-year-olds seemed daunting at first, but Sharneese was determined. The other assistant teachers in her classroom were initially dubious this would be anything but a disaster, perhaps envisioning children running off into a busy Flint street.

Sharneese began with building the children's stamina for walking and using the "rings"—the rope with colorful plastic rings. Each student keeps a hand on a ring, which helps them all stay together in a group because the rope is a concrete boundary the children can see. They would walk with the rope around the school building at first, and then over the bridge across the nearby river, and then through the campus, and then to the next street. Each day, they would go further and further, until Sharneese noticed their little legs and bodies giving out. Despite the Reggio philosophy of treating "children as capable," it wasn't always easy to convince her fellow teachers, or even herself, that the children were capable of the physical demands of a walk. Sharneese described one day in the fall when she decided to take the leap:

> I said, "All right y'all, I think it's time. I think we can cross [the campus]." The girls looked at me, they said, "You sure?" I said, "Nope, but we're going to try anyway." I said, "We won't know until we try." We walked around . . . and then there was one time we found the leaves . . . a leaves spot over there. And we'll go over there, play in the leaves for a little bit, and then they leave, and we head back to campus and say, "All right, y'all, we're getting closer and closer to the street. I think we can make it."

Safety is always an issue with taking students of any age on a walk, or to a site off campus and into the community for place-based learning. Even my secondary education students described safety concerns they had for their future teenage students as a possible barrier to place-based education. Sharneese and her assistant teachers had to reassure themselves of their children's capabilities and have trust in their students and their own teaching of expectations. Each successful walk that went a little further built that trust and Sharneese's confidence in her class. At the end of her story, she described the time she branched out to have the students cross a busy street to visit a park in downtown Flint.

> . . . they're young, of course I'm nervous to take them because they're all . . . I don't think anybody was barely even 2 just yet. I really get nervous because at that age, kids are really impulsive. But surprisingly, they were not. And so, of course, as we're walking, we sing before we cross the street. We have the "cross the street" song. We have, "you can stop look and listen before you cross the street. Use your eyes and ears before you use your feet." We'll sing that song

before we cross. I make sure the teachers have the friends' hands. I may have been a little nervous about crossing, so I made sure they had a teacher's hand.

Sharneese set the expectations for the walk with the children with a "cross the street" song and prepared for possible safety issues by assigning teachers to certain children. Once she trusted in her plans and her children, she was "surprised" how well they did—but she shouldn't have been. She had put in the work. Her confidence in her class inspired her to try visiting the Farmers' Market, which is across two busy streets on campus and downtown. Treating her children like the capable people they already are and can be with her guidance opened up a wide range of possibilities for learning from the environment.

These walks are important in Flint, in particular, where the prevailing narrative is that Flint is unsafe, dangerous, and violent. The data back up this narrative; in 2021, there were 67 homicides in Flint, a city of under 100,000 people. In 2021, the national average for murders per 100,000 people was 6.5 (Keefer, 2022; Stebbins, 2022). Guiding her students through a short walk in the city and on the college campus is introducing a counternarrative of Flint and allowing the children to generate their own narrative. To them, the city becomes a place of learning, a place to watch the water, feed geese, shop at the market, run around on a ramp, and play on the sculptures along the way. Including their voices adds to the experience of Flint beyond the stories of violence.

Flint Is the Third Teacher

Although Sharneese teaches 2-year-olds, there are standards and regular assessment practices that all classrooms at the ECDC work toward, reporting to families about their child's progress. The ECDC uses an assessment called Teaching Strategies (TS) Gold, which uses observation and documentation to report children's progress across several domains, including the academic subjects of literacy, math, science, and social studies. Sharneese spoke to me about all the objectives she was able to meet on her walks through campus, simply through some intentional questioning and activities. The children built their early literacy skills as Sharneese constantly asked them to describe what they were noticing on their walks, which is why the children were able to talk about "water" when shown a picture of the Flint River. Before one of their walks, Sharneese asked the class to guess what they might see on the walk, and to check and see if their predictions were correct. On campus, there is an artistic archway going over one of the sidewalks that has a circle formed out of bricks in the arch. Every time the class passed under it, Sharneese pointed out the circle shape, to the point where the children referred to the arch as the "round and round" when Sharneese showed a picture of it during morning group on a later day. She intentionally brought other round objects with her on one of the walks and stopped at the Circle Arch with the children for several minutes as they compared the shape of the arch to the objects she brought with her (Figure 5.2).

More exciting for me, as a social studies educator, I saw the beginnings of place-consciousness through early mapmaking activities. Ages 1 and 2 are much too young developmentally to create a map (Sobel, 1998), but what Sharneese did to meet the TS Gold Social Studies Domain "Demonstrates simple geographic knowledge" set the foundation for being able to meet mapmaking standards later. The children have a basic understanding of at least three of the five themes of geography (Gersmehl, 2014)—location (where they are in relation to their school), movement (people move to different locations), and place (describing a location based on its characteristics). One way that Sharneese introduced foundational mapmaking skills was the activity she did during the morning meeting I observed. To keep reviewing concepts after the walks are over, Sharneese shows pictures of landmarks they see on their walks to orient them to the location of places on campus. Sharneese chooses which landmarks to review based on what the students had interest in as they walked. One example is the large, multicolored social justice sculpture in the middle of campus. Many students at the ECDC call this work of art "Rainbow Rock" because of its many colors and design, which makes it ideal for climbing. Renaming the sculpture using their language builds place-consciousness as children become attached to the landmarks and can see themselves in the space.

Figure 5.2. *Sharneese's Class at the Circle Arch*

PRESCHOOLERS' NARRATIVES OF FLINT

Unsafe. Damaged. Poisoned. These words have been used to describe Flint even before the water crisis. Although the words aren't exactly false, they are limiting. Residents have been trying to change the narrative of Flint for a long time. In 2016, a Tumblr blog called "Most Violent City in America" shows peaceful, beautiful, or silly photos of the city with ironic captions to juxtapose the narrative of Flint as a violent place next to images of the "business as usual" of an urban center. Even among these competing narratives, the perspective from one particular group of Flint residents was/is missing—the perspective of Flint's children.

Flint's children are often seen by outsiders as a group deserving of pity—poisoned by their own government, in need of medical and educational interventions. See the previously mentioned cover of *Time* and the countless news articles and stories from 2016 as evidence of this. But I had doubts that the children of Flint saw themselves as "damaged" or saw their city as such. I thought about this idea one day when I picked Maggie up from the ECDC when she was about 3, and we met some friends at a restaurant in downtown Flint for dinner. We had to park a couple of blocks away and walk to the restaurant. It was a beautiful day, so I had no issues with taking my time on the short walk. Maggie ran a little way ahead to a bench on Saginaw Street, sat down, and exclaimed, "Look mom! There are benches on the street here!" She was so excited about the street bench that I took her picture sitting there (Figure 5.3). Behind her was a boarded-up building covered with graffiti and surrounded by barbed wire. Seeing my daughter's excitement over a bench

Figure 5.3. *Maggie's Bench on Saginaw Street*

on the street, while thoroughly enjoying a few minutes on a gorgeous day—and doing so despite the "ugly" surroundings behind her—made me think about her perspective on Flint.

Maggie was unaware of what had happened to her regarding the water crisis, and even now, she doesn't know or would not fully understand if I told her. She did not have the same experience as children who grew up and lived in Flint during the water crisis. Many children are very aware of what happened to them, as they still brush their teeth with bottled water, or watch their parents boil water before allowing them to bathe in it. Hana's students at Freeman were disgusted seeing a commercial where someone used water from the sink to rinse their mouths. Maggie's ECDC classmate told her that "water makes you sick," and I had to do my best to explain what they meant. Flint's children are aware of the water crisis—but do they see it as their deficit? Maggie sitting on that bench made me curious.

Ms. Jen's Reggio Preschool Classroom

There is no defined curriculum in the Reggio approach. Instead, the "curriculum is shaped according to the time [and] place . . . [with] freedom [for children] to express themselves and assess the world" (Arseven, 2014, p. 168). Drawing on social constructivist approaches, Loris Malaguzzi intentionally wanted students at the center of a Reggio classroom. Students create the curriculum, and teachers are there to set up an environment for them to create and discover. The vignette at the top of this chapter is from an experience designed by Jen Cozart, a Reggio preschool teacher at the ECDC. Jen's students are older than Sharneese's students (ages 3 to 5 in a mixed-age class), but Jen and Sharneese share a philosophy of using the city of Flint as an extension of the classroom environment. Because Jen's students are older than Sharneese's, she took her classroom on "explorations" of Flint more regularly. Because one of the roles of the teacher in a Reggio classroom is to document student learning, she often let students take on the role of "photographer." Jen would post these photos on her classroom Facebook page with captions as to what the class was exploring that day, what the students found interesting, and how parents could extend the students' learning at home to build on their curiosities.

The trip they took most frequently was to the Flint Farmers' Market, one of the closest places to the ECDC. Once at the market, Jen let her students browse picture books with the bookstore vendor and handle money to purchase a snack for the class. Sometimes they would eat their purchased snack across the street at Willson Park. I accompanied Jen's class on several of their trips to the Farmers' Market (and other places), and using photovoice methodology (Latz, 2017), I listened to the children's stories of Flint as prompted by the photos they took. The voice of the children impacted by the water crisis has been practically nonexistent (activist Mari Copeny,

"Little Miss Flint," being one major exception). Jen's students had a lot to say—but nothing about water! They spoke of the special places they encounter on their trips—a campus social justice sculpture (the same one Sharneese's students called Rainbow Rock), a statue of Gandhi in Willson Park, and the pedestrian bridge and its "cool shadows" (Figure 5.4).

Jen took her students to many places in Flint to provide them with educational experiences. She walked them to Flint's Cultural Center neighborhood, where they saw shows at the Longway Planetarium and the Whiting Auditorium and browsed the garden grounds of Applewood Estates, the famous C. S. Mott house. In the summer, the class often took their lunches to Willson Park for "Tunes at Noon," where live bands play in the park every day for the city to enjoy during a lunch break. Documenting and talking about these experiences were building the students' place-consciousness, an explicit awareness of their environment (Gruenewald, 2003a) and place attachment, a sense of belonging that is an extension of place-consciousness (Blankenship, 2018). Building both consciousness *and* attachment is important, as one can't work for change in a place they don't care about or know nothing about. The water crisis began with governments having no awareness or attachment to the people of Flint, which made it easier to dehumanize them and make poor decisions based on financial reasons instead of public health. These children were telling their own counternarrative, which was heavily intertwined with the places and stories of Flint not often told.

Figure 5.4. *The "Cool Shadows" of the Pedestrian Bridge Over the Flint River*

Mapping the Special Places of Flint

Because her students were interested in exploring their "special places" and taking these walking trips all over downtown Flint, Jen decided to co-construct the curriculum with her students in collaboration with the ECDC director, Joslyn. Every year, the ECDC hosts multiple outings for families to come see what the students have been learning Joslyn had expressed to her staff how the center was becoming too crowded for all the families to walk through (a good problem to have!), and that perhaps they could set up outside, or even in areas around campus. Jen and Joslyn then collaborated on a family night that would take families through the students' special places, which are often shared across classrooms. (As shown by the fact that both Sharneese's toddlers and Jen's preschoolers loved Rainbow Rock and running on the ramp in McKinnon Plaza—who wouldn't?)

Jen's preschoolers then set to creating a map of the "special places" of Flint that could be given to parents at the family night (Figure 5.5). Centers and activities would be set up at the special places so families could also be integrated into the community—but through the eyes of their children. Jen's class listed several places special to them on their walks, and even included some people on their map—Officer Bruce, the campus police officer assigned to the ECDC who often visited the students and helped them cross busy Chavez Street on some of their trips. The students also included "Mr. Mike," the groundskeeper at the center, who often waved to them from his lawnmower. Earlier in the school year, Jen had talked to the students

Figure 5.5. *The UM-Flint ECDC's "Special Places" Map*

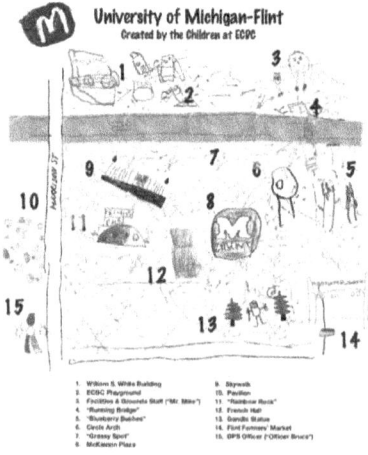

about what Mr. Mike does, including mowing the grass and keeping the sidewalks clear in the winter. They determined he was a special person and included him on the map.

The students then drew pictures/symbols of the special places and Jen helped them recount the "order" of when they reach these special places on their walks, to orient the students to location and direction. For example, they discussed that when they leave the building on their walks, the "first place" they pass is their own playground, then the pedestrian bridge across the Flint River, and so on. With Joslyn's help, they positioned their pictures on a map and added a key in the students' own language to describe the places. On family night, the parents traveled to these places where teachers and other classes had set up fun activities, including making collages underneath the Circle Arch on campus, sidewalk chalk in McKinnon Plaza (and running on the ramp, of course), and a dance party in Willson Park. The following fall, when Ms. Jen had some new students join her class, they used the map to orient new students to their special places and gave the map out to incoming freshmen during welcome week. Through Reggio exploration of place and expression of their own narratives in their own voices, the students shared the joy they have for Flint—even the old park benches. Perhaps a result of seeing the city through the stories of the children is that adults begin to see the potential for health, recreation, and joy in Flint as well (Dorfman & Kenney, 2020).

UNDERSTANDING REGGIO AS SOCIAL STUDIES INQUIRY

Watching both of my daughters learn through a Reggio approach at the ECDC fundamentally changed me as a scholar, and similar to much of my experience of motherhood, uncovered a lot of what I did not know and had not even considered. For years, as a social studies scholar, I studied inquiry-based instruction where students are the main drivers of investigation and instruction, ideally through close connection to the community. My dissertation work was with a teacher and her students who experienced a traditional economic business simulation more grounded in place and community than these experiences usually are. I wrote of the benefits and challenges to letting students drive the work, and ultimately the learning that students took away from the experience—not just in economics content but in their own place-consciousness and civic engagement (Whitlock, 2015, 2017). I've also written of the capacity for 1st-graders to take action on local and global issues important to them, and the role of the teacher in inspiring such action through questioning and curiosity (Whitlock & Brugar, 2017). In other words, I was primed to see the connections between Reggio and social studies, but it still took me somewhat by surprise as I saw Sharneese do a place-based social studies inquiry with my daughter

McKenzie, and watched Jen create a map using her students' interests in places.

Early childhood social studies scholars have written about children aged 4 to 7 engaging in the Inquiry Arc in various social studies disciplines. I use work by Payne (2015), Brillante and Mankiw (2015), Rogovin (2015), and Artman-Meeker and Kinder (2016) in my methods classes to show my preservice teachers real examples of high-quality social studies inquiry with young children. However, I also use the stories of Jen and Sharneese to illustrate explicit connections between Reggio Emilia, place-based education, and social studies inquiry.

For example, Dimension 1 of the Inquiry Arc (NCSS, 2013) helps teachers guide their students to writing their own inquiry questions rooted in their passions and interests. The Reggio philosophy is based on creating questions from student interests, and when Jen used her students' interests in their walks around Flint, she was making all these connections as she asked her class, "What are the special places in Flint?" "How can we show people these places?" and "What can we tell people about Flint?"

Dimensions 2 and 3 of the Inquiry Arc require teachers combining their knowledge of students and their disciplinary knowledge to provide their class with the sources and content knowledge they need to succeed in their inquiry. In the Reggio approach, knowledge of students is incredibly important. Sharneese showed this when she focused on safety during walks, but also in understanding that her class could rise to her expectations. Dimension 2 also focuses on disciplinary content specifically; both Sharneese and Jen engaged their students in learning developmentally appropriate concepts of geography, such as human–environment interaction, place, regions, culture, and location, direction, and mapmaking (NCSS, 2013). Sharneese also used her pedagogical content knowledge in mathematics and literacy to build her toddlers' vocabulary skills and emergent mathematical thinking.

Dimension 3 of the Inquiry Arc is about students engaging in sources that help them investigate their questions and curiosities. Social studies inquiry, like the Reggio philosophy, holds that teachers should be a guide for finding and developing sources, but ultimately students should be the main evaluators and analyzers of their sources. Like place-based educators, Sharneese and Jen showed their students that the city of Flint is a source of knowledge. Unlike the settler colonialist practice of "discovering" a wild forest, however, taking the classroom out into the city wasn't a practice of *using* the city for knowledge. Students were encouraged to express the story of their own reflections of the city—both how they shape Flint and how they are shaped by it—in their own words.

Dimension 4 focuses on taking informed action, helping teachers guide students toward real, authentic action that benefits their community (NCSS, 2013). Certainly, Jen and Sharneese made their students more informed and conscious of the assets of the city of Flint, and their action was to inform others of their story. The clear way the preschoolers took action was to create the "special places map" they gave to families during the ECDC family night. Since the map was also used in our university's welcome packet to new students, I would say their stories were at least out there to inform others of a different perspective (for more stories of Jen's students, see my 2020 article "Walking the City: Developing Place-Consciousness Through Inquiry"). Sharneese's plan was to walk her students to the Flint Farmers' Market to purchase fruit that they would make into smoothies. The students would then document the recipes to share with families. Unfortunately, COVID lockdowns hit right as Sharneese was planning this trip, and she never got the chance to complete the Inquiry Arc. In March 2020, the ECDC closed its doors for 18 months due to health and safety reasons from the pandemic. It was unclear whether the center would reopen, so Sharneese took another job. Her toddlers grew up and moved on, some to other childcare centers, as my daughter McKenzie did. Thankfully, the ECDC opened again in September 2021, and Sharneese's toddlers who returned were now entering Jen's preschool class. Walks into the city began again as the world reopened.

LEARNING FROM FLINT: A CALL TO RESEARCH AND PRACTICE

Social studies educators can learn quite a bit from the democratic, student-centered, place-based education happening in Reggio-inspired schools. Since the philosophy is used mostly in early childhood centers with students ages 2 to 6 years old, Reggio gets virtually no attention in the field of social studies education, being rarely implemented above preschool age. My UM-Flint colleague Christine Kenney collaborated with me on the design of the photovoice study in Jen's preschool class and aided in presenting some of the work at a place-based education conference. When I often dramatically exclaimed to her that "nobody" was writing about the connections of Reggio and place-based education in social studies, she just shook her head. Early childhood scholars have seen these connections for years. A simple Google Scholar search of Reggio and social studies yields many results from journals such as *Early Childhood Education Journal* and *Young Children*, as well as articles in the disciplines of art education and science education.

There are a few exceptions. One is Casey et al.'s (2019) student inquiry into a Reggio classroom around a community garden. Another exception is a study of a modified Reggio approach in a multi-age K–2 classroom and how students learned social studies through community walks and studying where their food came from (Christensen et al., 2006). In their article on the implementation of Reggio in a K–2 classroom, Christensen and colleagues (2006) wrote of the social studies that "permeate" in the Reggio approach:

Social studies exist in every fiber of this modified Reggio approach ... It permeates not only the environment, the interaction among parents, but also in the democratic ways in which social studies is studied and who contributes to curriculum development and to their ultimate goal of citizenship in a global society. (p. 17)

In her own words, Christensen explains that not only are students learning place-based social studies from Reggio-inspired classrooms, but the practice of implementing Reggio approaches models a democratic educational experience. So even when not explicitly teaching social studies content, the process of teaching with a place-based Reggio approach is still teaching social studies. More attention to the Reggio approach and its connections to place-based social studies would be an asset to social studies research, as would greater attention to early childhood social studies research in general, as it might give social studies researchers and educators more interdisciplinary conceptual frameworks to consider.

Social studies educators at all grade levels can employ what Sharneese and Jen did with toddlers and preschoolers in Flint to bring a Reggio-inspired approach to their classroom, particularly when it comes to exploring the community and allowing students to tell their own stories. Here are some possibilities:

- Take frequent walks with your students and give them the camera to document the trips. Allow them to take snapshots of what they see—not what we want them to see. Give students an opportunity to talk about their photography choices and identify why they took the photos they did, using their own words. If there is an opportunity to showcase their photos and their descriptions for the community, even better! Researchers could consider using this methodology, called photovoice (Latz, 2017), to honor participants' voices in qualitative research and disseminate their narratives in a public way.
- Students can express themselves in a hundred different ways (Malaguzzi, 1996), according to Reggio philosophy. Although Jen's students took photos and Sharneese had plans for her students to create recipes, Carrie Mattern, a high school English teacher at Carman-Ainsworth High School in Flint, had her students write poems inspired by the many murals painted around the city by various artists. Carrie's students chose a mural that spoke to them and responded with poems that are beautiful reflections on their relationships with the city and growing up in Flint. Carrie partnered with the Flint Public Art project to publish the poems on the Pixel Stix app. Residents walking the city and viewing the murals can scan a QR code on a plaque near a mural and read the

students' poems on the app. In an article for Flintbeat (Nesbitt, 2022), Mattern is quoted as saying, "It's always been an important objective for me as an educator to have students write for authentic audiences rather than just me . . . It was also critical that my students create community by writing for, and about, their community."

My daughter Maggie eventually had Ms. Jen for preschool, before the COVID lockdowns began, and she continued to take her students around the city. Years later, after the COVID lockdowns had lifted but long after Maggie had left the ECDC, I was driving Maggie in downtown Flint regularly every day for therapy appointments. One of our traditions was to guess the color of the weather ball as we drove by it on the highway. On one of the trips, I decided to take a detour down Saginaw Street to get closer to the weather ball. As we drove along the bricks on Saginaw, Maggie laughed uncontrollably about the bumpy ride, which gave me an opportunity to explain to her the uniqueness of the bricks to the city. Long after Maggie no longer had memories of Ms. Jen or her preschool classmates, she kept those memories of the city and her joy for the little things in the community, which opened the possibility for learning history. But perhaps more importantly, seeing Flint through her eyes always reminds me of other possibilities of resilience and joy.

CHAPTER 6

Montessori for Flint

In graduate school, I worked with undergraduate teacher preparation students placed in Montessori classrooms for their social studies field placement. After giving myself a crash course on Montessori methods (which in my experience had not been discussed much, if at all, in my own teacher preparation journey), I saw connections with Maria Montessori's philosophy and the philosophies of inquiry instruction I taught in my methods courses.

Montessori education shares many similarities to the Reggio Emilia approach. The Montessori approach was also developed in 20th-century Italy, by Dr. Maria Montessori, a physician and an educator. Montessori began a school for underprivileged children in Italy and studied an educational approach based in child development psychology that she believed worked best. The Montessori method, like Reggio, values students as capable beings who deserve extended time to pursue their interests (with small groups if they so choose) with their teacher as a guide. Montessori believes the environment is also incredibly important, and that students should have access to specific materials that will aid their learning.

Whereas the Reggio approach has no specific curriculum (it is developed from students and community in a specific place), Montessori has a structured curriculum based on large "cosmic" questions that have students ponder where they fit within a community and what their larger responsibilities are to a global society (Stephenson, 1997). Reggio classrooms don't typically extend into later elementary grades, whereas Montessori classrooms can exist through high school. Montessori education also has strong connections to place-based education, albeit in different ways than Reggio. In this chapter, I look at Montessori as a type of place-based education, especially in how Montessori education attempts to address spatial injustices in places that adopt the philosophy in their schools.

Many Montessori schools are tuition-based private preschools. In the Flint area, Grand Blanc Montessori in the suburbs of Flint costs families approximately $7,000 per year, per student (Private School Review, 2023). What public options exist for Flint children? This chapter describes how a group of parents successfully navigated the complexities of Flint Community Schools to open a public Montessori school-within-a-school at an elementary school in Flint, but also the challenges they faced which were/are not unique to Flint.

MONTESSORI'S CONNECTIONS TO PLACE-BASED EDUCATION

Montessori education was developed by Maria Montessori in 1906. Through observation of children at her Casa dei Bambini school in Rome, she discovered that the children, previously deemed unruly and incapable of learning, were most engaged when given long periods of time to explore what they were interested in learning. Montessori noticed that students learn from their surroundings, so she designed the environment to aid their learning. A Montessori curriculum is highly structured, with specifically designed learning materials such as movable alphabet letters, classification cards, and a checkerboard for mathematical learning. Part of the Montessori method is that students learn practical life skills, such as preparing meals and cleaning, and how to complete these tasks independently. Maria Montessori was quite protective of her methods, initially choosing to personally train Montessori educators (Murray et al., 2020), which may have prevented her methods from spreading beyond Italy in the beginning.

When she published *The Montessori Method* in 1912, the movement spread to the United States. However, instead of being an option for the most disadvantaged children, Montessori schools became sought by the wealthy American elite. The American Montessori Society says that Maria Montessori found that Americans were faithful to her methods, but others say she was disappointed in the "Americanized version" of Montessori (Murray et al., 2020). Montessori education fell out of fashion partially due to William Heard Kilpatrick, a progressive-era scholar. Although Kilpatrick had positive things to say about Montessori education, he criticized the structured nature of the approach. Whereas Montessori believed in a specifically prepared environment to aid in learning, Kilpatrick (like Dewey before him) believed that students should learn from the real world and real experiences, rather than an environment prepared by a teacher. He was excited to see that students were learning "life skills" such as serving food and cleaning up after themselves but wondered if the community's needs should dictate which "life skills" are important to learn. Kilpatrick also bemoaned the lack of play, stories, and art he observed in Montessori classrooms (Kilpatrick, 1914).

Although at odds in their fundamental beliefs, both Montessori and Kilpatrick believed that students learned from their environment. It might be easy to connect Kilpatrick's project method (1918) to place-based education today, as he described more specifically the community as the extension of the classroom. However, Montessori's philosophy isn't as far from place-based education as Kilpatrick's opposition would make it seem. Although Montessori believed in "liberty through a *prepared* environment" (my emphasis), part of the Montessori curriculum guides students through an examination of self and one's place in the world (Stephenson, 1997, p. 54). Students aged 6 through 12 study the "cosmic curriculum," where they learn about the universe and reflect on their role in it. Montessori wrote that schooling should contribute to students' development of self, "orientated to [their] environment, adapted to [their] time, place, and culture" (Stephenson, 1997, p. 54). This examination of self is part of place-based education, as Gruenewald (2003a) explains that we are shaped by our environments just as much as we do the shaping.

A large element of the Montessori approach is peace education, which is indicative of Montessori's belief in making the universe a better place to live—shaping our world in a more just way. When the Montessori method was reinvigorated in the United States in the 1950s and 1960s, resulting in the formation of the American Montessori Society, many Montessori schools (public and private) took on an aspect of social justice education, heavily rooted in community. As one Montessori administrator from a 2016 study commented, "Montessori asserts that, to truly serve the whole child, we must see him or her in context. What happens with a child inside a classroom cannot be disconnected from what happens in his or her neighborhood, and beyond" (Banks & Maixner, 2016, p. 9). To this administrator, Montessori education requires school leaders to be aware of and address systemic injustices that impact students and communities (Banks & Maixner, 2016).

THE BENEFITS OF A PUBLIC MONTESSORI EDUCATION

The mid-century resurgence of Montessori education in the United States coincided with the Civil Rights Movement in the United States and the fight for integrating public schools. As we saw in Chapter 4, access to quality early childhood education and childcare for working families leads to positive outcomes for all children, especially those living in poverty (Heckman & Karapakula, 2019). Lack of access to early childhood education became one of the spatial injustices the Civil Rights Movement sought to rectify. Black parents during this time became leaders of Montessori schools, as they wanted a place for their children to understand and reflect on their place in the universe in a way that affirmed them and built them up—something a systemically racist public school environment could not provide (Debs, 2019).

One such parent was Roslyn Williams, a mother in Harlem who participated in a parent-led Montessori program that bussed Black children to white Montessori schools. When that program was defunded, Williams and other parents formed their own racially integrated Montessori preschool in Harlem. Their school was ahead of its time, accepting students with physical and intellectual disabilities, which was rare for the time, and branching into Montessori teacher preparation (Murray et al., 2020). Mae Arlene Gadpaille was another influential Black leader in Montessori education, opening a Montessori Education Center in 1964 in Boston. Gadpaille dreamed big—she envisioned a community Montessori school with a Black neighborhood built around it, something like the vision of Frank Manley. Although those plans didn't come to pass, her other big dream—access to Montessori education for all students—did have a lasting impact. After years of local fundraising and putting up thousands of dollars of her own money, Gadpaille successfully campaigned to the United States Senate to have Montessori education funded by public Head Start (Murray et al., 2020).

Once Montessori education became part of public Head Start programs, many public Montessori magnet schools were created within already existing public school systems. Seen as an alternative to poor public schools, magnet schools in general are created around a theme (environmentalism, performing arts, and STEM are some examples). In the 1970s and 1980s, Montessori magnet schools became popular in urban areas—Denver (Trierweiler, 2014; Urioste, 2014) and Kansas City (Murray et al., 2021) have examples of successful Montessori schools with racially diverse student bodies. As of 2015, 56% of students in public Montessori schools were students of color, and 47% were on free and reduced lunch (Debs, 2015). The creation of public Montessori schools opened access to an approach previously accessible primarily to white students of wealthy, educated parents.

Research shows that Montessori education leads to positive outcomes for students, particularly for Black children in the United States. In general, investing in public early childhood education leads to greater gains for economically disadvantaged students (Heckman, 2012). The increase of preschool attendance in Flint during and after the water crisis is one example (GFHC & PPHI, 2023). Investing in Montessori education may reduce disciplinary issues, particularly among Black boys. The focus on peace education in Montessori prioritizes a communal culture of working through conflicts, rather than suspensions and expulsions (Debs & Brown, 2017). The practice of continuous observation of children may help Montessori educators remediate instruction and attend to students who need support, potentially avoiding an inappropriate special education diagnosis for students, particularly for Black boys, who are disproportionately referred for special education services (Jor'dan, 2018). Jor'dan (2018) writes that this same observational practice can help educators understand and cultivate the "genius of African American children" (p. 2), something Roslyn Williams and her fellow Harlem parents understood during the Civil Rights Movement.

CHALLENGES FOR PUBLIC MONTESSORI

Despite the benefits of public access to Montessori education, any public school is beholden to the inefficiencies and deficiencies that define the American public school system. Public Montessori schools are not immune to issues related to standardized testing, accountability measures, systemic racism, and bureaucracy.

Accountability Era and Montessori

Many have surmised that the Montessori method as described by Maria Montessori in the early 20th century is incompatible with the accountability movement of the early 21st century. For public schools to receive state funding, students must take the state standardized testing and be subject to the state's accountability system. In Michigan, for example, teachers are ranked on an effectiveness scale (Highly Effective, Effective, Minimally Effective, Ineffective) determined by administrator classroom observations and student growth on state assessments. Ratings by school are public and can impact aspects of a teacher's employment and certification if given numerous poor rankings. Strict accountability measures tied to school funding, public ratings, and performance can naturally lead to an abundance of test preparation in schools, which has been heavily documented, especially in the field of social studies, which has been disappearing in elementary classrooms due to test preparation (Burroughs, 2002; Heafner et al., 2006). Montessori methods are the opposite of test preparation—but it's possible that administrators in states like Michigan may feel the pressure to sway from the Montessori method to get a better effectiveness rating. If schools truly believe in Montessori education as a form of place-based education, they'll need to trust in the community to provide the learning their students need. This is much easier said than done.

Starletta is an American Montessori Society–certified Montessori teacher. In her wealth of experience in early childhood settings in Flint (public and private), she has seen what she calls "Montessori in name only," meaning that schools or classrooms claim to use the approach but don't faithfully follow it. However, Starletta doesn't necessarily believe that is a bad thing—if teachers use some of the methods but not all, she believes this is still providing children access to Montessori benefits. That said, Montessori-trained teachers like Starletta can become frustrated when a school's mission of Montessori education drifts away to meet accountability requirements (Murray et al., 2020).

Do Montessori Schools Address or Create Spatial Injustices?

Many public Montessori schools were developed as magnet schools because of desegregation orders, and many of them successfully became more racially diverse. Often, white parents would bring their children into Black neighborhoods for school because the Montessori school was located there (and vice versa), as was the case with Roslyn Williams in Harlem in the 1960s and in Family Star Montessori and Mitchell Montessori Schools in Denver (Trierweiler, 2014; Urioste, 2014), which successfully integrated their preschools after desegregation orders in the 1990s.

However, these same school districts often annulled their desegregation rules and policies, which challenged the existence of some public Montessori schools. With no mandates in place, districts often chose to consolidate schools or return to the neighborhood school model, which can be more racially segregated. This also happened in Denver with both schools; as budgets were cut and desegregation orders were no longer enforced, parents in these communities fought hard to retain Montessori education for their children, even if it meant physically moving to different neighborhoods (Trierweiler, 2014; Urioste, 2014). In the early 2000s, the Kansas City Missouri School District attempted to consolidate their Montessori schools to save money, which also caused parents to voice their concerns. Although the consolidation plan didn't pass, it caused distrust between Montessori parents and the district (Murray et al., 2020), leading to parents enrolling their children in other charter schools. On the flip side, Montessori schools in primarily low-income Black neighborhoods can become gentrified when white families move in to be closer to the school. Public Montessori schools can address spatial injustices, but also create them, as all public schools are created under racist systems.

The "study of self" in Montessori is another example of how a Montessori education can create injustices as well as address them. Students don't leave their race at the door of a Montessori class, and an examination of self and social identities within the curriculum means that Black students and other students of color will need to address the racism they experience in their lives. Students in Montessori classrooms are not immune to racism just because a school is thriving with a diverse population. This examination of self can go south quickly if the Montessori teacher has not engaged in their own "study of self" and their relationship to racism—experiencing it or upholding it. This is especially important as the population of students in Montessori classrooms become more racially diverse (Debs, 2015) but the population of Montessori teachers do not. Like many early childhood and elementary teachers, as of 2019 Montessori teachers are mostly women (91%, according to Zippia.com, a career website) and mostly white (73% per Zippia.com). The American Montessori Society now features anti-bias, anti-racist (ABAR) professional development for Montessori teachers to engage in a 12-week "study of self" in which they engage in "transformative discussions" and "strive to deepen commitment to liberation and living out the fundamental tenets of Montessori education" (American Montessori Society, n.d.).

The Instability of Public Education

Public Montessori schools can suffer from public school instability as well, not unlike the instability of Flint Community Schools (FCS) described in Chapter 3. The Denver and Kansas City Montessori schools described in articles by Trierweiler (2014), Urioste (2014), and Murray and colleagues (2020), all faced challenges from the instability of their public school system, and all required parents to be vocal and challenge the system, and/or leave their beloved school. A Kansas City parent was quoted in the *Public School Montessorian* (2005) as saying "[Families] are not leaving because of a bad experience. They are afraid [the school] is not going to be here much longer" (p. 14). Instability in leadership of a school district isn't ideal for cultivating community connections, which are necessary in effective place-based education, Montessori or otherwise (Oakes et al., 2017).

MONTESSORI FOR FLINT

According to Jor'dan (2018), Michigan is among the states with the highest concentration of public Montessori schools in the country (p. 2). However, it wasn't easy for me to find options for public Montessori schools in the Flint area. One public charter school, International Academy of Flint, appeared in my Google search for "public Montessori in Flint," and although their website describes students learning in multi-age groups as occurs in Montessori classrooms, no mention of "Montessori" exists on their website. In 2015, a group of parents in Flint set out to address the lack of public Montessori options.

Elizabeth Jordan and Heather Laube both have sons who attended Alpha Kids, a tuition-based Montessori preschool run out of the YWCA in Flint. Elizabeth is a Flint native who works in the nonprofit sector, whereas Heather is a sociology professor at the University of Michigan-Flint. When I spoke to them about their journey opening a Montessori school in Flint, they kept singing the praises of Ms. Deb, a Montessori educator who worked for Alpha Kids. Both of their sons had such a good experience with Ms. Deb that she single-handedly sold Elizabeth and Heather on the promise of Montessori education for their children. However, in 2015, Alpha Kids closed its doors; its building was demolished to make way for more affordable housing downtown. Elizabeth, Heather, and a group of parents from Alpha Kids decided to homeschool their children together as a group in Heather's house. Heather purchased some of the Montessori materials from Alpha Kids (and some was donated to them), and Heather even hired Ms. Deb! The parents re-created the Montessori experience in Heather's attic, considering what their options would be when their children were ready to start kindergarten. The parents wanted to continue their children's Montessori education but were faced with limited choices.

Elizabeth decided to investigate what it would take to get FCS to offer a Montessori program. She started by reaching out to then superintendent Bilal Tawaab, inviting him to join a meeting of other parents interested in a Montessori option. Both Heather and Elizabeth stressed to me how important it was to this parent group that they work *with* FCS to provide a Montessori education, rather than try to open their own charter school. One could presume that opening your own charter school is a far more intense, expensive, and lengthy process for parents with no expertise in public school operations (and with their own full-time jobs), and these parents wanted something more immediate that their children could attend when it was time for them to enroll in kindergarten. However, being a Flint native who also works in the city, Elizabeth was determined to invest in the community and wanted to send her son to Flint schools rather than send him outside the city.

Surprisingly, Superintendent Tawaab responded to Elizabeth's meeting invitation and joined the parents in talks about opening a Montessori classroom. I use the word "surprisingly" because at this same time (early 2016), Superintendent Tawaab was inundated with media requests and donations stemming from the world attention to the water crisis. And as we saw in Chapter 3, Dr. Grace, the Pierce Elementary School principal who worked with Superintendent Tawaab at the time, said that his only priority was making sure schools had clean water. During this time, I was coordinating student teaching placements in Flint elementary schools such as Freeman Elementary and Durant-Tuuri-Mott Elementary. Our Center for Education Preparation had tried numerous times to get ahold of Dr. Tawaab, unsuccessfully. A few months later, we heard from him—when he was asking to redo our affiliation agreements and was rethinking the partnership between University of Michigan-Flint and FCS. So, when Elizabeth said that getting Superintendent Tawaab to show up to her meeting was as simple as inviting him, I was legitimately surprised.

Elizabeth wasn't all that surprised. She said that Dr. Tawaab was incredibly interested in early childhood education, specifically Montessori education. She said he was very supportive of opening a Montessori classroom and knew that the principal of Durant-Tuuri Mott Elementary school would be equally supportive. That building had spare classrooms and could house the new Montessori program in FCS. Elizabeth also believed that Dr. Tawaab really wanted to meet with parents in the city, especially parents of prospective students, and that he was a believer that Montessori education would be helpful for Flint's children impacted by the water crisis, and perhaps even attract families to Flint schools given the lack of Montessori options in the area.

Both Dr. Tawaab and the Durant-Tuuri-Mott principal gave the Montessori parents their word that a Montessori classroom would open in the building the following fall. The parents assumed that the school district would take care of everything—advertising for enrollment, hiring teachers, and so on. However, giving the green light was apparently where a lot of their involvement ended. The parent group, calling themselves "Montessori for Flint," wanted to be involved in their idea but ended up running the entire program. They toured other public Montessori schools, purchased more materials with their own money, and recruited families and students on their own. The parents also did manual labor—cleaning the space in the building, painting lockers, and moving furniture. Elizabeth said that district offices whose help they needed with teacher hiring and student enrollment were often unresponsive. As the school year approached, students were enrolled in the first K–1 Montessori classroom in FCS, but there was nobody to teach them. Again, the parents took over. Heather reached out to me and asked if we had any recent graduates or student teachers from our education programs who would be willing to be trained in Montessori methods. She also talked to Alpha Montessori teachers she and Elizabeth knew. Just 90 minutes before "Meet the Teacher" night, a teacher was hired for the classroom.

Eventually, the parents, particularly Elizabeth, got into the groove of running the Montessori for Flint program. Capitalizing on her experience in the nonprofit sector, Elizabeth applied for and received grants from the Welch Foundation and the Flint Community Foundation to fund and expand the program in future years. She built an enrollment website that she shared with FCS, and she recruited families just as she would recruit customers or "business prospects." Elizabeth was amazed that the school district didn't have this infrastructure set up already, and that the school district was content to let the parents completely take over operations of the classrooms. Due to their tireless efforts and unpaid labor, the program did expand—adding a K–2 classroom and a preschool classroom. Two of my former students who student-taught at Freeman—one of whom was Starletta (from Chapter 4)—became Montessori teachers there and enjoyed their experiences.

But, as mentioned in Chapter 3, Superintendent Tawaab was fired in 2018. When new superintendent Derrick Lopez took over, the parents weren't so sure they had his support to continue the program. Despite the parents doing the bulk of the work, the program relied on the space at Durant-Tuuri-Mott, as well as crucial funding and infrastructure to operate. The parents spent a lot of time justifying their existence, inviting Dr. Lopez and the board of education to join them in meetings, but this time they weren't as successful. Ultimately, the program was allowed to continue, but only at the eleventh hour. The following year—same thing. The Montessori for Flint program was not immune to the effects of the instability of FCS.

In Chapter 3, I described the instability of FCS—their revolving door of superintendents and a fractured board of education. Because Montessori for Flint was a part of FCS, they suffered from the instability as well. The parents relied on structures of the district to hire and pay teachers and enroll students, and even to continue the program at all, which became a source of stress with each new superintendent to the point that Elizabeth, Heather, and other parents moved their children to other districts for more stability. They could never be sure the Flint Montessori classrooms would be open the following year. Heather enrolled her son in a project-based learning magnet school through Grand Blanc Public Schools outside of Flint. Elizabeth, still committed to a Montessori education for her son, drove him to a school in Waterford 30 miles away.

The inefficiencies of FCS also meant the program wasn't advertised as well as it could be. Elizabeth, coming from a business mindset, wondered why the school district didn't send more information about Montessori for Flint to all preschools in the surrounding areas, or advertise in neighboring districts to attract more students. Certainly, the water crisis added to the instability of FCS, and perhaps advertising for the Montessori classrooms was not a high priority. Elizabeth and Heather both felt this was a missed opportunity—that Montessori education in Flint could have been seen as beneficial for children impacted by the water crisis. This is what they thought Bilal Tawaab believed when he agreed to start the school within a school. But after he was gone, the vision was lost.

Nonetheless, despite the instability year to year, the Montessori for Flint program continued to grow. As of this writing, there is now a Montessori hallway at Durant-Tuuri-Mott with a preschool classroom, two lower elementary classrooms, and an upper elementary classroom. During the pandemic, the Montessori teachers delivered materials to their families' homes so they could continue a virtual Montessori experience. Elizabeth no longer runs the operations of the school, but she commented that her name and phone number must continue to appear on some documentation because she still gets calls from interested families from time to time, some of whom are not from Flint. This is what the Montessori for Flint parents hoped would be the case when they expressed the desire to work with the public school system instead of opening their own private or charter school. Elizabeth mentioned parents from Grand Blanc calling to enroll their students in Flint, which seemed virtually unheard of. She says that although the program should be considered successful, the lack of follow-through and implementation from FCS prevented it from growing bigger. There are parents who send their kids to the Montessori classrooms that wouldn't have enrolled in FCS otherwise, which could have had a tremendous impact on education in the city.

LEARNING FROM FLINT: INCORPORATING MONTESSORI ELEMENTS

Despite the many challenges to public Montessori programs, there are clear benefits for children who learn with the Montessori method. Debs and

Brown (2017) and Jor'dan (2018) have written about the academic and social benefits for Black children specifically, and the American Montessori Society website boasts of many successful entrepreneurs, entertainers, and athletes who were once Montessori students. But is Montessori education place-based? One could argue it isn't place-based given the methods and curriculum are the same no matter where the Montessori education takes place, which is in opposition to the idea that a place-based curriculum comes from local knowledge (Sobel, 2005). The success of many Montessori schools is because parents can come from many different places to attend, which perhaps gives schools a more diverse, integrated population.

I would argue that Montessori classrooms certainly have elements of place-based education. Teaching children how to learn about themselves and their place in the world, globally or locally, is an important part of place-consciousness (Gruenewald, 2003a). The toddlers and preschoolers walking around Flint described in Chapter 4 were learning about themselves—the things they like and that interest them, in relationship to place. The cosmic Montessori questions of "Who am I? Do I have a role to play in this wondrous universe?" (Stephenson, 1997, p. 57) for me implies that students need to be action-oriented to their world and thinking about their role as citizens, perhaps even justice-oriented citizens. Maria Montessori believed in learning from place, even if she thought she should construct the place herself with her materials. What can we learn from the parents' attempt at Montessori education in Flint or from the Montessori method itself? Much of it has to do with the basic themes of Montessori education and how those can appear in "traditional" public school classrooms through social studies. My former student Starletta said she saw a lot of Montessori in "name only" but didn't find that to necessarily be a bad thing. Starletta is a "Young 5s" teacher in Grand Blanc who said she was hired because of her Montessori experience and because the principal at the school wanted to bring Montessori practices to her public school. Many of these practices, such as those listed below, are quite compatible with place-based education and justice-oriented social studies.

- Bring big, "cosmic" questions into your curricula—social studies is a great place to consider compelling questions such as *Who am I?* and *Where am I?* and have them connect to content in the early grades. In Michigan, one of the state standards in 1st grade is to examine a family story told by two different generations. To meet this standard, students can certainly examine themselves, their families, culture, traditions, place . . . all while understanding what historical sources are.
- Allow students to work more in smaller groups or individually, conducting inquiries on topics that concern or interest them. There's no reason why a teacher can't help cultivate ideas (as Kilpatrick

would prefer), but students can still own what is most relevant for them to learn. In my dissertation, I studied a traditional economics simulation where students had a lot of control over the social issue they were addressing with their business models. The curriculum I co-designed could not be considered "Montessori" in the slightest, but it did feature significant student choice and independent work, with minimal (but not zero) guidance from the teacher. Students in my study were able to learn economics content on their own while building their civic awareness (Whitlock, 2017).

When the Montessori for Flint parents decided to leave their own Montessori creation, where did their children go? What other options existed for a school that incorporates elements of Montessori education they loved that was still a public school? Prior to 2019, there wouldn't be too many options for these parents. But then a charter school opened in the Cultural Center neighborhood of Flint that promised an education rooted in place and the culture of Flint. And families were very ready to be a part of it.

CHAPTER 7

Flint's Place-Based Charter School

In August 2015, UM-Flint welcomed David Sobel to Flint. Sobel has written at length about place-based education (Smith & Sobel, 2010; Sobel, 2005), and we were inspired by his work when we were designing our place-based secondary education program, which was set to launch with its first course in the fall. During his visit, he met with faculty to talk about curriculum design, he spoke with community members and support staff at our university, and he rode his bike on the Flint River trail. He liked to ride his bike to explore places he had never been, he said. Later, when I read his book *Mapmaking with Children: Sense-of-Place Education for the Elementary Years* (1998), I chuckled to myself, as he recommended allowing children to explore places on their bikes as a crucial part of developing their sense of place. However, Sobel's primary purpose in Flint was to be the keynote speaker at the Our Cities, Our Classrooms conference—a small, professional development opportunity for teachers hosted by the Genesee Intermediate School District.

During his keynote speech, Sobel used a metaphor that has stuck with me since, and I often use it to describe how I conceptualize place-based education in my own work. He described place-based education as the "terroir" of teaching. I had never heard the term "terroir," and when he explained it, I realized why. Terroir refers to the specific taste and flavor of wine that is made from a specific region. Factors such as the climate, soil, and topography of where the grapes for the wine are grown make each bottle of wine a unique stamp of time and place. I had never been a wine enthusiast, but I vaguely knew this idea. He likened place-based education to the terroir—the specific place and time where our students "grow" and where we as educators "grow" affects our flavor and makes us unique.

Sobel went on to describe the opposite of terroir—boxed Franzia wine or cheap stuff like Boone's Farm (sadly, this was more in line with my knowledge of wine). Such wines are mass-produced and taste and smell the same no matter where or when you buy them. They always taste the same and are completely devoid of any singular place. These wines serve a different purpose—efficiency, familiarity, lack of risk, lack of expense. This isn't necessarily bad if any of these is your objective when drinking wine, but no one would call Franzia a fine wine. For a robust experience, you need to embrace the terroir.

This analogy resonated with me because I immediately thought of the time in my career when I worked for a for-profit charter school management company—National Heritage Academies (NHA). I started my career in education teaching kindergarten, and then mostly middle school social studies at Vanderbilt Academy, one of NHA's K–8 charter schools in Holland, Michigan. At the time I taught there, I knew NHA was a "chain" of sorts—they had schools in Grand Rapids and another one in Holland on the other side of town. However, Vanderbilt never really felt like part of a chain. Located in downtown Holland, we served the same population of students as the local elementary school. Charter schools are public schools, so they must follow the same state regulations with testing, and from my understanding, received the same per-pupil funding that all public schools in Michigan received, but without funding from property taxes. As a first-year teacher, I didn't think about or question where the other money came from for NHA to fund their schools. To me, I had the same struggles as any first-year teacher in an underfunded school in a high-poverty area. As a white teacher with primarily Latinx students, I was in the mix of unlearning institutionalized racism and sexism, figuring out what type of teacher I wanted to be, and developing my content knowledge to make me a better social studies teacher.

I spent five years at Vanderbilt Academy and met lifelong friends. I loved my students, experienced joy nearly every day, and learned so much from them. Vanderbilt was one of the first schools that NHA opened, before they had developed many of their systems, and my principal at Vanderbilt ignored many of NHA's corporate mandates to homogenize education. The school building itself was not like NHA's other carbon-copied franchise schools. Although the parking lot flooded in a rainstorm, internet service was spotty at best, and it had oddly shaped classrooms, the school was part of the community. Near a beloved area downtown called Washington Square, it was on the parade route for the Holland Tulip Festival. Teaching there, I felt part of the community.

The website for any NHA school looks the same. On their website, they describe a charter school's purpose: "When individuals want an option available other than a district public school, they may opt to propose a charter to their state authorizing agency. The community leaders, parents, teachers, principals, or businesses create a charter." This description, if done like this, would mean that community members would see a need in their own community on how they would like their children to be educated and build their own school from the ground up. This is not unlike what the Reggio Emilia community did post–World War II. And there are schools in Michigan that have done this—but not NHA. NHA would use market research to target urban areas where school systems were struggling to give parents another option. NHA would search for community members who would be willing to set up a board, offering to take care of all the work for them to start the school as long as it was part of the NHA brand. For anyone optimistic about charter schools being community driven, for-profit management wipes all that away. At best, NHA was astroturfing charter schools—making them look like grassroots initiatives when each school was meticulously planned for maximum profit by a corporation.

In 1994, then Governor John Engler signed the Michigan Charter School Act into effect at the same time as Proposal A was passed, which changed Michigan's school-funding model to a combination of per-pupil funding and property taxes rather than property taxes alone (Dwyer, 2014). This combination allowed groups like NHA to flourish in Michigan, as they opened charter schools and took money from the state. NHA describes their role on their schools' websites: "the management firm often provides central support to a number of schools, so each individual school can focus their energy on teaching and learning." This description conveniently declines to mention that as a management firm, NHA takes a significant cut of the state funding given to each school they open to provide this service. Although it is entirely possible that charter schools can be created as place-based and community focused, there are other schools that exist because of their belief that place and community are precisely the problem. NHA banks on the fact that there will be families who are unhappy with the public school system and believe a corporation could create an environment for a better education. Instead of investing resources in the public school system to make it a more viable choice, it invests in a cheaper, shinier version. To extend Sobel's analogy, rather than cultivate the environment to grow grapes for fine wine, many for-profit companies like NHA opt for the Boone's Farm. It's easier and cheaper.

SCHOOL OF CHOICE IN FLINT

In 1999, NHA opened two schools in the Flint area. They joined two others that opened in the late 1990s and early 2000s. When Governor Rick Snyder removed the cap on charter schools in 2011, four more charter schools opened in Flint. Not all these schools make use of a management company, and not all of them are for profit. They had varying levels of success. If one measures success by achievement scores, the two NHA schools are not performing much better than Flint Community Schools (FCS) in reading and math (*Public School Review,* 2023a, 2023b). Enrollment in the two NHA schools has also remained about the same since 1999.

Charter schools are not the only "choice" option in Flint or in the state of Michigan. In 1996, Michigan passed a schools-of-choice law, which allowed students to attend any public school in the state, not just your own neighborhood school. Now that property taxes didn't account for all the school funding in Michigan, schools could get some state money for any student who enrolled there, regardless of where in Michigan they lived. In

Flint, so many districts are adjacent to the city that students who live in Flint don't necessarily have to attend FCS. And they don't—enrollment in FCS has declined 66% over the last 10 years (Goetz, 2022e), whereas some districts surrounding Flint have grown. For example, Westwood Heights in Mt. Morris Township northwest of Flint city limits has doubled in size over the same time period (Goetz, 2022e).

Another choice for Flint families is to homeschool their children. Michigan has no regulations on homeschooling, except that you must be the guardian of the child you're homeschooling. This puts Michigan toward the top in the country in number of children homeschooled. In 2018, approximately 49,000 students in Michigan were homeschooled, although that number could be much higher since parents are not required to report they're homeschooling their children (Bondy, 2019). Of course, during the COVID-19 pandemic, homeschooling rates skyrocketed, increasing from 5% of children to nearly 11% of Michigan children being homeschooled (Walker, 2021). In metropolitan areas like Flint and Detroit, that number increased up to 12 percentage points (Walker, 2021). Evidence indicates that some of these children are returning to traditional public schooling now that the pandemic has abated (Levin, 2022), but not in FCS. Enrollment is still in decline at the time of this writing and expecting to drop further (Goetz, 2022e). Even before the pandemic, Black families have been choosing to homeschool their children due to their extreme distrust of oppressive school systems (Mazama, 2016), but most homeschooling remains the choice of well-educated parents with at least one college degree. There is evidence that Black children who are homeschooled score above the 50th percentile on achievement testing, suggesting that a better school environment with more parental and community involvement is helping Black children succeed (Ray, 2015).

Another growing choice for parents in Flint is a new charter school that opened in 2019—the Flint Cultural Center Academy (FCCA). For the entire year of 2019, I heard of so much promise about this new school. I watched the building construction on my way to work every day—the building was right downtown off I-475 in the Cultural Center neighborhood of Flint.

FLINT CULTURAL CENTER: A LONGTIME GEM

The Flint Cultural Center is a physical space taking a few blocks along Kearsley Street in Flint northeast of I-475. The land was owned by the Flint Board of Education in 1947, when C. S. Mott donated some land adjacent in hopes of putting a branch of the University of Michigan there—the city's first 4-year college. Although this would become a reality 10 years later, in the meantime another group of wealthy Flint residents, including Michael Gorman, then editor of the *Flint Journal*, wanted to develop the cultural scene in the city known for its industry (Azizian, 2008).

Gorman took the lead and organized a massive, city-wide fundraising effort along with donations from General Motors (GM) and C. S. Mott to build several museums and performing arts venues in the area. Construction on these buildings began in 1958. By this time, the Flint Board of Education had successfully opened the Flint Junior College nearby, and C. S. Mott donated millions for the opening of Flint Senior College of the University of Michigan. This relatively small area of Flint was now home to two colleges and a host of cultural venues—all managed by the Flint Board of Education, further intertwining school and community. Although the Flint Senior College eventually became the University of Michigan-Flint and moved to a location downtown on the Flint River, the rest of the Cultural Center remained and even expanded. In the 1990s, the Flint Board of Education turned over operations to a newly created Flint Cultural Center Corporation (FCCC), which now manages the properties there. The Flint Cultural Center organizations are the Flint Institute of Art and the Flint Institute of Music, the Flint Repertory Theatre, the Whiting Auditorium, the Longway Planetarium, and the Sloan Museum of Discovery (Flint Cultural Center, 2022). At the end of Kearsley Street is Applewood Estate, the historic home of the Mott family. The Gloria Coles Flint Public Library is also in this area, although not managed by the FCCC (Azizian, 2008). The Cultural Center still relies heavily on fundraising and donors for operation, although Flint residents passed an arts millage in 2018 to help supplement funds. Genesee County residents can get into the Flint Institute of Art and the Sloan Museum for free, and other events are heavily discounted (Jackson, 2018). The consistent monetary support from residents dating back to the 1950s shows how important this area is to the city.

When the Flint Board of Education was managing the Flint Cultural Center, there was a deeper connection between the cultural institutions and Flint schools. Pierce Elementary, where Dr. Grace (from Chapter 3) is principal, still claims to be a performing arts magnet school due to its proximity to the Cultural Center and its prior connection to the area, there isn't much of a partnership anymore. The Mott Foundation, a regular donor to the Flint Cultural Center, saw the lack of a partnership between the informal education spaces in the Cultural Center and FCS as a missed opportunity. As has been documented in earlier chapters, the relationship between FCS and the Mott Foundation is fraught at best. Also, considering that the Flint Board of Education has been trying to close Pierce Elementary, its closest school to the Cultural Center, it doesn't appear that a partnership is on the horizon.

FLINT CULTURAL CENTER ACADEMY

The leadership of the Mott Foundation approached Eric Lieske, the superintendent of schools in nearby Davison, about opening a charter school right in the middle of the Flint Cultural Center. It was the foundation's desire that this school be one of the institutions within the Center and use the buildings there as extensions of the school. The board of education for this school would start with members from the FCCC to ensure collaborative efforts in the design and the curriculum of the school. Renovations of the Flint Public Library and Sloan Museum were being planned, so students at this new school would get to use new, refreshed cultural spaces daily. The foundation leadership asked Eric if he knew anyone from his years working as a superintendent who would be a good principal for this new school.

Recounting this story to me later, Eric explained to the Mott Foundation that opening a self-managed charter school would require a school leader-who had experience in a variety of aspects of running a full school district, not just someone who had been a principal at one school. The sheer number of details, from applying for the charter to ordering the furniture, would have to be led by one person. So that one person needed a wide range of experiences. Eric said he would think about recommendations for the Mott Foundation and get back to them. Within a few weeks, he was taking the job himself. Eric spearheaded huge initiatives in Davison, such as a balanced calendar and standards-based grading. He thought that working with the Cultural Center and the Mott Foundation to open a school would be a great opportunity for a new challenge. Once the charter had been approved, with Grand Valley State University as its authorizer, the school was announced to the public, with Eric attached as "Principal/CEO." In 2018, construction on the school began in an open parking lot in the Cultural Center, funded entirely by the Mott Foundation.

Almost immediately after this announcement, parents in Flint began to take notice. For starters, it was hard to ignore the beautiful, bright-colored building being erected right off I-475. The building was being painted bright yellow, which stood out on even the dreariest Michigan winter days. The other parents at the ECDC whose children were in Maggie's class began to ask me what I thought of the new school and whether it might be a good spot to send our kids for kindergarten. Other parents I knew at UM-Flint were excited about the possibility of this brand-new school so close to our workplace we could walk there. I sensed their enthusiasm over the school's proposed integration with the Cultural Center. Perhaps they were nostalgic, remembering attending shows at the Whiting or the Longway Planetarium, and now excited at the possibility of those places being part of their child's education.

I lived in Clarkston, about 20 miles south of Flint. I was planning to send Maggie to Clarkston Schools, which seemed perfectly fine to me, and the bus would pick her up at our house. I was getting a little burned out taking both of my daughters to work every day with me, and putting them in school in Flint or in a school other than my neighborhood school had never occurred to me. But for Flint parents, the choice of kindergarten was a real dilemma. Parents I talked to who lived in Flint seemed pretty set against sending their children to any elementary school in FCS. So much so that it was almost a given in any conversation—FCS was never an option. I don't think many of the parents I talked to knew about Montessori for Flint, and even the Montessori parents were looking for other options as the program was constantly in flux with Flint schools (see Chapter 6).

FCCA opened in the fall of 2019. The demand was huge. There were 375 open spots in the school, K–5 (it later expanded to K–8), and 1,100 students had entered the school's lottery. The buzz for the new school continued, and enrollment grew the next year as well (Goetz, 2022e). In the spring of 2020, when Maggie and her classmates were nearing the end of their time at the ECDC, all I heard about from parents was the lottery, and the backup choices if their child didn't get into the new school. My experience at NHA had left me skeptical of all charter schools, so I had trouble getting behind the enthusiasm. The school's announced mission and vision seemed to be very place-based and rooted in Flint. It appeared that students would truly get to experience the "terroir" of the city, and that this school would really be different from other charter schools. But I wasn't optimistic.

A DAY AT THE FLINT CULTURAL CENTER ACADEMY

I planned to visit FCCA in my early research stages for this book. However, just past the midway point of its first year, the COVID-19 pandemic hit the world, and like many schools in the spring of 2020, FCCA went virtual. Eric Lieske believed that FCCA was well equipped for the move to virtual instruction. Students were already provided with their own devices, which they could use to participate in synchronous instruction. In the fall of 2020, FCCA returned to in-person teaching with strict COVID protocols in place and some students still choosing to attend virtually. Although many schools in the area did return to some in-person instruction at some point during fall 2020, FCS did not return to in-person instruction until nearly 18 months later, in early 2022, another piece that set FCCA apart from the rest of Flint. Partially due to the pandemic, I did not get a chance to visit FCCA until January of 2023.

As I pulled into the parking lot, which the school shares with the Sloan Museum, it was incredibly clear that I had entered a completely different educational space than when I used to pull into Freeman Elementary to visit student teachers. I had to put five (yes, five) new tires on my car in one year due to the potholes in Freeman's parking lot. This parking lot was freshly painted, completely plowed from a recent snowfall, and pothole free. The front office where I checked in was surrounded by windows. Although I couldn't immediately see Eric Lieske's office, the other administrative staff offices were enclosed in glass, and I could see two students happily meeting with a staff member inside. Another small boy was waiting in the office, apparently having just arrived at school. The administrative assistant told the boy his class was at the Flint Institute of Music attending an event with the Flint Youth Symphony Orchestra, and a security guard arrived to escort the boy there. Eric came out of his office for our meeting, happy and smiling. It all looked amazing—the new building, the casualness with which the students were out in the community learning from the Flint Institute of Music, and the excited school leader who agreed to show me around.

Eric kindly offered me a cup of coffee as we sat down in his office to talk. The sign on his desk identifying him as "Principal/CEO" was cringeworthy for me as it reminded me of my time at corporate NHA. I remembered that a lot of NHA schools were brand new and shiny too—designed to dazzle prospective families. I was determined to see for myself how the vision for FCCA was being put into practice. I was determined not to be dazzled by fresh paint, but also to be open minded and put my NHA experience and charter school bias aside. During my half day visit there, I did learn a lot about how FCCA was perhaps building on Frank Manley's vision for community schools, while simultaneously missing some obvious opportunities to be more connected within the city. Thanks to Eric's willingness to share his experience, I also learned of his belief in the school's tremendous potential for growth.

Education in the Community

As described in Chapter 2, Frank Manley wanted to extend the school experience out into the community of Flint. Buildings were open late, there were classes for adults and families, and neighborhood events. Very little attention was paid to the reciprocity of this. What did Flint have to offer our schools? The initial vision of FCCA was that it would be a member of the Flint Cultural Center and partner with those spaces to give students an education in the community. This idea shows the students that Flint has much to offer students, both inside and outside of the classroom. And abundant evidence suggests that this is happening as planned.

For example, FCCA has no school library of its own. Instead, students walk to the Gloria Coles Flint Public Library to check out books, which means they must get their own library card, setting them up for future visits to that space. There are no official music teachers or art teachers at FCCA. Instead, students take classes at the Flint Institute of Art and the Flint Institute of Music. During a tour of the building, Eric took me to a hallway that connects to the Flint Institute of Music, and I walked in on some 3rd-grade students taking a dance class. Eric spoke of how important it was that students aren't given exclusive access to these spaces. They attend classes or check out books during hours that the buildings are open, which means students regularly interact with community members who just so happen to be at the library or the art museum at the time. Such exposure can provide students with a sense of place consciousness and an ability to see themselves as belonging in these spaces (Gruenewald, 2003a).

Missed Opportunities

Despite the many ways the students interact with the Cultural Center, Eric mentioned how much more they could be doing within the city. Flint is of course much bigger than the Cultural Center neighborhood, and FCCA students come from all over the city and surrounding suburbs. Place-based education has deep roots in environmental education (Demarest, 2015), as well as social studies education/geography (Sobel, 2005), so social studies and science are two school subjects with potential to give FCCA students the opportunity for further learning in city. At FCCA, there is an incredible amount of potential for inquiry in these subjects, as the Longway Planetarium and Sloan Museum are part of the Cultural Center. Certainly, they can provide materials and resources needed for community learning.

Eric sees the collaboration between the Longway, Sloan, and FCCA teachers as at the beginning of a journey toward a robust partnership. The Longway Planetarium often brings in employees to do science lessons with the students, but the collaboration between these educators and classroom teachers needs more time to develop. Collaboration with the Sloan Museum has had even less time to come to fruition, as the museum had been under renovation since before FCCA opened, reopening in July 2022. Part of the renovation included a connecting hallway to FCCA. On my tour, Eric opened the door to the Sloan Museum and we were literally in the middle of one of their exhibits. Now that the museum is open, he hopes students will be able to visit the museum more often, making use of this community educational space.

Since FCCA opened, the school was able to embed the connection with the fine, visual, and performing arts buildings in the Cultural Center and the Gloria Coles Flint Public Library immediately. The channel for place-based education with science and social studies education is still being developed. Given that these subjects are often overlooked at the elementary level everywhere, not just charter schools (Dilberti et al., 2023), this is not entirely surprising to me. But a place-based school not investing in social studies and science when they are literally in the backyard of great community resources is a clearly missed opportunity, but perhaps one that is on its way to being something great.

Collaborating With Contemporaries

I asked Eric about his relationship with FCS, and he chose his words carefully. Eric doesn't believe that FCCA is in competition with FCS, although that's easy to say when they have been growing in enrollment and FCS has not. Eric even mentioned how he had a collegial relationship with Anita Steward, the former superintendent of FCS. They spoke frequently about the similarities in their work; Anita was a new superintendent, and even though Eric had years of experience as a superintendent in Davison, he was new to being a school leader in an urban area.

What I took from his constructed answer was that FCCA is focused on their mission and vision for a quality educational experience connected to the community. This is what makes them a unique and attractive option for families. His relationship with Anita indicated they had no problem collaborating, perhaps seeing collaboration as mutually beneficial. This is a rare situation, particularly in Flint. In a recent case study of a separate Flint charter school, Tenneriello (2022) found that the school was trying to play catch-up by constantly reacting and adapting to what other public schools in the area were doing, rather than working with each other. It appears that Eric and Anita wanted to try something new.

As discussed in Chapter 3, Anita's apparent willingness to collaborate with competitors and the Mott Foundation was precisely what the Flint Board of Education did not want. But after the recent election in fall 2022 where the Flint Board of Education saw four new members elected, Eric was optimistic about the future of collaborations.

LEARNING FROM FLINT: SCHOOLWIDE PLACE-BASED EDUCATION

Overall, I would say FCCA impressed me more than I thought it would, but mostly in its design and intention rather than in its execution, although there is potential on that end as well. I was incredibly skeptical about a school founded and initially funded through philanthropy, but the Mott Foundation's vision for a school intertwined within the Cultural Center has certainly been realized. Physically and philosophically, FCCA is uniquely Flint. It is connected to the area in ways that some students from Flint may not have seen, experiencing arts and culture in authentic settings from educators throughout the community, not just the ones they see at school. However, the school does not yet appear to be utilizing the full potential of the Cultural Center. Collaborations have been with a few institutions more than others, and students haven't explored the performing arts community of Flint beyond their immediate surroundings. I'm not completely discouraged. The school's COVID protocols over the course of the pandemic no doubt prohibited a lot of community exploration. The renovation of the Sloan Museum of Discovery and the Gloria Coles Flint Public Library has also slowed possible community collaborations. I am confident that the Mott Foundation will see their vision fully realized, as Eric Lieske, their

"CEO" understands it so clearly. Here are my takeaways from my visit to FCCA regarding schoolwide implementation with a place-based focus:

- Although students at FCCA are making good use of the Cultural Center neighborhood, the arts community in Flint extends far beyond this area. I hope in the future that students at FCCA can collaborate with other art galleries in the city, or with mural artists who are creating art all over the city. Place-based education is local, but such a narrow focus on formalized institutions in a specific geographic radius can be limiting. Although it may be easier and tempting for a school to focus on one neighborhood, students miss out on larger connections.
- Students at FCCA are certainly learning from Flint. A possibility for the future would be to apply what they've learned back into the community. Could students design an exhibit at the Flint Institute of Art? Might they weigh in on what shows and performances the city should offer? Or even advocate for Cultural Center funding to Flint residents and the city council? Taking informed action can be a great way to develop the reciprocal relationship between school and community and give students practice in working with community organizations to determine need.
- Now that it is open, the Sloan Museum has potential to be an impactful education experience for social studies inquiry. Artifacts of Flint's history are literally connected to the school, making sourcing these local inquiries even easier. There is also the Whaley House Museum—an 1880s house from Flint's prominent Whaley family (they gave Billy Durant his first loan to start General Motors) has been historically re-created and is within walking distance of the Cultural Center. Yes, use local museums as educative spaces, even holding classes there when possible, but also allow your students to critique these spaces and to work with museums to showcase counternarratives of place.

It is possible that charter schools can be more than just a cookie-cutter, Boone's Farm option of public schools that enter communities devoid of context to disrupt the present history of schooling and take advantages of public resources. FCCA was created to build on Flint's resources, work with these informal educational spaces as teams, and even be open to collaboration with FCS. FCCA still needs time post-pandemic to age like fine wine, but the potential is there. I get hints of the terroir.

Part III

HOW CAN TEACHER PREPARATION BE PLACE-BASED?

CHAPTER 8

Place-Based Teacher Education in Flint

"This place is haunted, right?" I asked Jacquie as she swung open a large door. I was joking, but Jacquie answered me seriously.

"Oh, I'm sure it is. I've definitely felt people here as I worked late at night. But I think they're friendly." Jacquie stated this so matter-of-factly that for a moment I believed in ghosts as much as I believed her when she said this house was built in 1872. As we walked through the open door, she explained that this part of the Stockton House had once been a hospital. The room had been re-created to look like a hospital room from the 1920s, which considering Jacquie's comment about ghosts, was now quite unsettling.

On this particular day in the spring of 2016, I was attending a work meeting at the Stockton House Museum where Jacquie (the teacher at Freeman Elementary from Chapter 2) was a member of the board of directors. Several middle and high school teachers from Flint and some surrounding school districts were meeting with secondary education professors from the University of Michigan-Flint to collaborate about the newly implemented place-based secondary education program at the university. We had taught one year of the new program so far and were looking into what was working and what wasn't working, as well as planning for the upcoming courses that hadn't been offered yet. As was usual practice, we did this alongside the secondary teachers who welcomed our students into their classrooms and/or teamed up with us to participate in community projects. We often liked to meet out in the city rather than at the university, so Jacquie, a member of our group, offered up the Stockton House.

It's rare in academia to say one enjoys going to meetings, but I *loved* these meetings. I enjoyed working with the secondary teachers—they were lovely people with great ideas and a perspective I rarely got to hear being at a university. I also loved whatever spot was chosen for our meetings because I got to know new places in Flint. The Stockton House, as I learned from Jacquie as she gave us a tour, was built in 1872 by Thomas and Maria Stockton. Maria Stockton was the daughter of the first settler in Flint, Jacob Smith, and was quite wealthy as a result. She inherited the land on which the Stockton House was built, and she and her husband, Thomas, a Civil War colonel, settled there after the war. The Stocktons were well known in Flint, and they often entertained other Civil War veterans at the house—both Union and Confederate. Maria's wealth contributed to the opening of the first public library in Flint (one of the first in Michigan), as well as land for the Michigan School for the Deaf (which remains open next to its original spot).

After a couple of generations of Stocktons lived there, the house was sold to the Sisters of St. Joseph's, who added on to the house and turned a large part of it into a hospital in the 1920s. After being treated, patients would spend their recovery time in the parlor of the house. The house eventually became abandoned, until being repurchased for historical restoration in 2002 and opening as a public museum in the city. The house sits on a natural spring and wetland, which was cleaned up and reopened to the public to walk through in 2013. And, according to Jacquie, the house is haunted.

This meeting was my first visit to the Stockton House, and really my first time exploring the Grand Traverse neighborhood, an area full of unique Victorian mansions built in the 1850s–1870s. Later, Jacquie's historical knowledge of the area inspired me to consider the Stockton House as a future destination for a community-based activity in my methods course. If our meeting had not been held at the house, I would never have learned of its interesting place in Flint's history.

I relate this story about my first time at the Stockton House as an example of how being a part of a teacher education program dedicated to place-based education fundamentally informed my own learning and scholarship. Right before I came to Flint as a professor, I had written my dissertation on an elementary economics curriculum that took a traditional market simulation and added an element of civic engagement and community engagement (Whitlock, 2015; Whitlock & Fox, 2014). Although my dissertation was deeply rooted in place-based education, I can only say that after the fact. The phrase "place-based education" does not appear in my dissertation.

When I got to Flint, the secondary teacher educators saw my scholarship connecting to the work they were doing to redesign their secondary programs into place-based teacher education. They invited me into their course design and planning and immersed me into scholarship that now informs how I look at my own research and teaching. Although the practice of inquiry was common in social studies education, NCSS's College, Career, and Civic Life Framework (C3) had only just been published as I started in Flint in 2013. As I became more familiar with the C3 Framework, and as it became more well known and used in social studies, I developed more of an understanding of place-based inquiry. Those first few years in Flint I felt as if I were drinking from a fire hose as my own conceptions of place-based education and place-based teacher education converged with new understandings of environmental injustice from the water crisis and new knowledge of Flint. I often left meetings with the secondary education group renewed, inspired, and hopeful. My time with Jacquie and the Stockton House ghosts was one such day.

This chapter focuses on how the secondary teacher educators envisioned place-based teacher education at UM-Flint, and how teaching courses in this program that were not specifically social studies informed how I approached teaching my own elementary social studies methods courses (which I describe in the following chapter).

PLACE-BASED TEACHER EDUCATION

Place-based teacher education (PBTE) is built on a foundation of place-based education and other related concepts, such as culturally sustaining (Paris & Alim, 2014) and culturally responsive pedagogy (Ladson-Billings, 1995). Other concepts related to place-based education are funds of knowledge (Moll et al., 1992) and community cultural wealth (Yosso, 2005). Noel (2016) describes culturally relevant pedagogy, funds of knowledge, and community cultural wealth as the "theoretical basis" for place-based teacher education. All these concepts involve understanding one's students and what they bring to the classroom—both their assets and their challenges. And these concepts involve reflection by the teachers on what they bring to the classroom—their own experiences and biases. Martell and Stevens (2019) looked at how social studies teachers specifically used culturally sustaining pedagogy in their teaching, in hopes of highlighting models for preservice teachers to see. What they found is an importance of teacher reflection on their place in the community and the importance of providing examples for in-service and preservice teachers of what culturally sustaining pedagogy looks like locally. Place-based education includes an examination of place on the development of the self (for both students and teachers), so it makes sense that place-based teacher education would need to include knowledge of these concepts/theories as well as opportunities for reflection.

Although understanding these foundational concepts is incredibly important, PBTE needs more than just exposing preservice teachers to theory and reflection. Most teacher educators would agree that teacher preparation of any kind can't solely take place in a university classroom—students need to go out into schools to apply the theories and strategies they have learned. PBTE is no different, but with the addition that communities and places where the schools exist shouldn't be ignored either. And students also need practical applications of how to connect the school and the community. Zygmunt and Clark (2016) described the practice of preservice teachers jumping into field placements with no understanding of community as "guerrilla teaching" (p. 3). The use of the word "guerrilla" here draws images of teachers quickly dropping into field placements, ambushing students with one-off lessons required by professors, and moving on. PBTE requires a much more intentional, long-term relationship between the teacher preparation program, the K–12 schools, and the community.

For example, Noel (2016) recommends a "community of practice" (Lave & Wenger, 1991) among teacher educators, K–12 educators, and community partners in which all of these groups are considered "teacher educators," not just university faculty. Together, this community of practice would plan program and course outcomes, deciding how much, where, and when preservice teachers will be learning in the community. Although university faculty tend to monopolize decision making when it comes to curriculum, since they must be the ones to seek approvals from university curriculum committees and state Departments of Education, Noel (2016) recommends involving other teacher educators into these processes as much as possible to ensure equity.

As far as what the preservice teachers experience in PBTE, Dani (2019) recommends involving preservice teachers in the work of addressing community issues that are important to community members to help preservice teachers find relevance in the curriculum they're required to teach and help them see the "so what." She cites the rationales from Zeichner (2010) and Cochran-Smith (1991), two leading scholars in teacher preparation, who argue that context- and community-specific teacher education can foster teachers who are justice-oriented change agents in their communities.

Michigan has a tradition of supporting teachers and teacher educators in place-based education through the Great Lakes Stewardship Initiative (GLSI). The GLSI puts on professional development and helps educators design place-based inquiries. The GLSI has hubs in communities across the state to further contextualize the support it provides. Eastern Michigan University (EMU) in Ypsilanti is the hub site of the Southeast Michigan Stewardship (SEMIS) Coalition. With this support, EMU created a teacher preparation program based on the concepts of deep inquiry, connections to the city of Detroit, and informed civic engagement. This effort required pedagogical shifts for faculty, as they had to (re)think their teacher education practices being less about program completion and more about creating a learning community (Lowenstein et al., 2018). These shifts included thinking about inquiry as negotiated with students and the community, where teacher candidates apply disciplinary learning in a local context. It involved shifting the concept of "community" to be beyond the university classroom and focusing on "careful and prolonged observation" of place (Lowenstein et al., 2018, p. 42). It also involved shifting from thinking about civic engagement as abstracted from community to deeply connected to community. The planning and discussions were a collaborative effort with university faculty, teacher candidates, practicing teachers and administrators, and community members. But this was not a simple task; it took time to build trust among these groups and to come to agreement on what PBTE would look like in southeast Michigan.

The EMU secondary teacher preparation program is a block of courses that all meet on the same day to allow for collaboration and field experiences. These courses include a curriculum methods course in subject areas, a school-based field practicum where students work directly with students, and a social foundations course centered on environmental justice. It was important to the planning group that EMU's teacher preparation program be embedded within community transformation and social justice work already happening in Detroit. One such way is for teacher candidates to get involved in professional development through the SEMIS Coalition or the GLSI to connect with other place-based educators (Lowenstein et al., 2018).

Flint also has a hub of the GLSI called Discovering Place, which partnered closely with UM-Flint as we were developing our PBTE program. Our mutual relationship with the GLSI allowed us to connect with EMU faculty during our process, and they served as place-based "mentors" of sorts as we grappled with many of the same decisions as they did. When I came to Flint, our secondary PBTE program was moving from planning phase to implementation phase—and I jumped right in.

UNIQUELY FLINT

During most of my time at UM-Flint, the early childhood and elementary teacher preparation programs were housed in the Education Department. The secondary teacher preparation programs were in the College of Arts and Sciences, spread out among departments based on subject area. For interdisciplinary subjects like science and social studies, a department from one of those integrated disciplines housed that particular secondary program. (For example, for a while at UM-Flint, the secondary social studies program was out of the Political Science Department, who then had to collaborate with the departments of history, economics, sociology, etc.). Since both the elementary and secondary programs needed to be accredited together and were evaluated by the state of Michigan as one whole "ecosystem" (a phrase commonly used by the Michigan Department of Education), it required the Education Department and representatives from the College of Arts and Sciences to regularly meet and collaborate. When I got to UM-Flint, this large group met monthly, calling themselves the "Education Unit."

Among the first discussions I took part in in the Education Unit meetings was a plan for a complete overhaul of all the secondary teacher preparation programs. At the time, secondary teacher candidates essentially earned a degree in a content area, applied to their education program to complete general teaching methods courses, and then jumped into student-teaching. It was the guerrilla teaching mentioned above—a quick drop into the Education Department for a semester, and then out into the classroom (Zygmunt & Clark, 2016). The Education Unit wanted a more integrated study of education concepts such as equity and diversity, development and learning, and student engagement that started right from the beginning of the secondary program. They believed teacher candidates should be in the field much sooner and think of themselves as education students much more quickly. A committee was made to design the new approach to secondary teacher education, led by Suzanne Knight, an English education professor in the English Department.

The "redesign committee" included people from many departments in the College of Arts and Sciences, as well as representatives from the Education Department and secondary teachers in Flint. Their desire was to make a teacher preparation program that was "uniquely Flint" and be anchored in place-based education. The idea was the program would have teacher candidates frequently engaging in reflection of their relationship to Flint, examining how the place informed their teaching journey, while also recognizing all that they needed to continue learning about the city. They would do this in a block of courses that they would take spread out over their program (not all at once in the last semester before student teaching), and these courses would spiral learning about education issues and concepts relevant to Flint while getting candidates out into the city with community partnerships to work regularly with middle and high school students.

In my first semester at UM-Flint, the redesign team shared an expansive document that outlined the proposal for the program idea. This document outlined the philosophy of what PBTE could look like in Flint. The second page of the document declared that the committee "sought to create a place-based professional program that was 'uniquely Flint,' where Flint itself would frame the program." Also near the front of the document was the following statement, which convinced me that taking the job at UM-Flint was the correct choice:

> While knowledge of and participation in any community is imperative, we kept returning to the idea that we wanted candidates to be more than participants. We wanted candidates to be activists. Therefore, we wanted a program that would instill and nurture candidates' dispositions to engage in equitable classroom practices and to be agents of effective change in their profession and community.

I already believed in place-based education for K–12 students; this document didn't have to convince me. For example, I had already taught my preservice teachers about concepts related to place-based education for years in graduate school. I used examples from my dissertation data collection to discuss project-based learning with a civic engagement component. I taught them about inquiry as an instructional practice, and we practiced finding sources that would allow students to investigate questions important to them. I required my students to create a profile of the community where they were going for their field placements so they could better understand their students' cultural backgrounds. We even went on a field trip to the Michigan Historical Museum. It was easy for me to assume that I was "already doing" place-based education. After reading this document, I realized that what I was doing was teaching these future educators *about* place-based education. I wasn't actually *teaching through* place. This was an important, career-changing realization for me. Perhaps learning to teach in Flint is different from learning to teach anywhere else, just as K–12 students in Flint are different from everywhere else. I was excited to follow this new line of learning.

That same fall, the redesign team presented their philosophical document and proposal for the new secondary program to the Education Unit. The ideas that secondary teacher candidates would be in the field earlier and take education courses earlier meant that the collaboration (or lack of it) between the Education Department and College of Arts and Sciences needed adjustment as well. The redesign committee also had a vision that the block of courses would be co-taught by faculty in both schools, so the logistics of faculty appointments and course loads needed to be figured out. The redesign team also wanted the block of secondary education courses to have a new course prefix called "SEC"—but which department in the College of Arts and Sciences would staff these courses became a question because the courses were to be taught across departments and schools. The Dean of the School of Education and Human Services proposed a new office called the "Center for Educator Preparation" (CEP) that would help staff the SEC courses, make field placements (previously done by the Education Department), lead the Education Unit, and continue to make connections to community partners and schools.

I received my first shock of what higher education meetings were like when, to my surprise, nobody wanted to discuss the philosophical foundations of the new program. All anyone was interested in were the logistics, and how the redesign document didn't specifically outline (nor did the team figure out) the issues of staffing, course loads, and reporting lines. Most of the hesitation to give the program a vote of confidence came from some of my colleagues in the Education Department, who had recently redesigned the elementary teacher preparation program. Their redesign was a much different process—proposing a few new courses and a reorganization of the sequence of some old ones. I sensed that the ambitious scale of the secondary redesign was overwhelming for some. I also got the impression that there were "turf wars" over course ownership and processes that needed to be ironed out. For example, the Education Unit wasn't a governing academic unit, so could it approve programs? It looked as if the new secondary program would be killed before it started.

I was so intrigued by the possibilities to learn from this program, these courses, and this experience that I decided to shoot my shot. In one of my first faculty meetings, I argued that if we agreed that the foundational philosophy of PBTE was what we wanted, then we should approve the program and figure out the logistics later. I could tell there was a distinct undercurrent of distrust that the logistics *wouldn't* get figured out, or that the work would fall on a select few, or that as a new professor I had no idea what I was talking about. However, the new secondary programs were approved with a caveat that there be a new team formed to deal with logistics—the "implementation team." And to nobody's surprise, everyone was in favor of the vocal newbie being on this team.

And so began my journey in planning and implementing a PBTE program that was "uniquely Flint," navigating the complexities of university structures and working with the Flint community. In addition to logistics, from 2015–2019 I taught every one of the SEC courses that made up the place-based block at least once, in addition to supervising student teachers. Although these courses were not "social studies" courses per se, they were very much connected to social studies through their focus on learning through place-based inquiry. I learned more about Flint by teaching these courses than anything else I did. In the following sections, I describe how each of the SEC courses I taught was an example of my experience working in a PBTE program, including co-teaching, the benefits of working with a partner school district, and the challenges of having courses meet directly in a school.

CO-TEACHING

The first SEC course I taught was titled "Community, Family, Self." I felt comfortable with this being the first secondary course I taught because concepts of identity, family, and culture have been part of my elementary social studies methods courses and I thought I could adapt a lot of what I did before with secondary students. I co-taught this course with Danielle De La Mare, a communications professor who also advised secondary education students seeking a teachable minor in Speech. We also had help from our University Outreach office in planning the place-based elements of the course. They connected us with a neighborhood association in Flint—the South Parks Neighborhood Association—who were looking for a class to partner with on a project.

Danielle and I met in late summer 2015 with South Parks residents at their community center, and it soon became evident that exactly what they wanted our students to do was not clear at all. They spoke of their disappointment that there were no "young people" in the neighborhood anymore after school closings and a reorganization of community centers in the city. In the 1970s, the South Parks neighborhood hosted massive block parties with carnival rides right on Thread Lake. The residents, many of them elderly, wanted to get the neighborhood back to a livelier time. Although I enjoyed hearing from the residents, after the meeting I was panicked. How were we going to develop a course based on a project when we had no clue what this project was? Danielle was not fazed. She seemed content to have most of the syllabus wide open, to take things day by day, and to stay in contact with the South Parks people to guide us.

My panic in comparison to Danielle's unflappable demeanor was just one example of how different we were as educators. One of Danielle's areas of expertise was mindfulness. She often led sessions for faculty in meetings and with our students. I think this made her an introspective, calm, thoughtful educator. She would enter our classroom quietly and calmly to start class. Contrast this with me: I tell corny jokes and make outdated pop culture references. I am also highly caffeinated and *loud*. Everything about this class and teaching with Danielle was outside my comfort zone, which was ironic since this was the class I thought would be the most comfortable teaching. Perhaps it was the pressure of teaching the first class in this new place-based program, or that I fought so hard for its approval, but I really wanted this course to succeed. I don't remember exactly when I decided to just embrace the discomfort. It was something I felt I needed to do, and I trusted Danielle.

My co-teaching experience with Danielle taught me that there are a lot of ways to be a teacher educator. For example, I was always flexible with my students in a course when things weren't working, or I needed to adjust due dates or assignments, but I never set out with blank spots on my syllabus like we did for "Community, Family, Self." But when I kept an open mind and tried it, it went exactly as Danielle predicted—ultimately our students learned from the South Parks residents in an authentic way. There were bumps and stresses but nothing we couldn't figure out. I also learned so much from our University Outreach team who connected us with the South Parks residents. In addition to matching us up with a great community partner, they taught me interactive mapping tools with Google so that I could show my students how to make an asset map that was shareable and editable. Sara McDonnell spent hours with me on this small element of how to improve my course assignment; it was as if I took a mini-course from her at the same time as I was teaching. I like to think Danielle learned from me as well. I showed her the generic rubric I used and tailored for reflection assignments, such as the final reflection paper we required. She was excited to try grading with rubrics that were shared with the students, and I think it made the students' final reflections more comprehensive when they had a guide.

I approached co-teaching with Danielle as an opportunity to learn from someone new and get out of my comfort zone, but I also learned that I bring specific strengths to teaching, and that embracing those enhances the experience as well. The idea in the original intent in the design of co-teaching in the program was for students to learn from different perspectives, and I think my students got that each time I was paired with someone to teach a course. Additionally, my students also got the benefit of the "behind the scenes" work of teacher education with all the support behind the secondary program from university and community groups. Co-teaching, whether it was with faculty members or community members, or both, was always an opportunity for me to reflect on the kind of place-based educator I was and wanted to be.

SCHOOL CULTURE SHOCK

Like many teacher preparation programs, our students needed to complete field experiences in schools where they could study teaching methods and student learning alongside mentor teachers. In the fall of 2018, I taught a class called "Seminar in Methods" with my colleague Laura McLeman. This was designed to be the class where students have an extensive field experience prior to student teaching. We got to know Linda Heck, a special education teacher at Flint Southwestern High School, through the Discovering Place program. Linda frequently engaged her students in place-based education, particularly around a duck habitat near the high school. Laura and I were interested in having our students learn from a special education teacher. UM-Flint didn't have a special education program, and our secondary students received very little knowledge on how to adapt content for exceptionalities. If our students spent time in Linda's classroom, not only would they be seeing special education, they would be seeing that place-based education was possible in special education classrooms.

Flint Southwestern High School allowed us to use a conference room in the school where our class could meet, and Laura and I decided to truly immerse our students in the school and have every class meet there. We often began each class in that conference room and then made our way down to Linda's class as a group. Our students were required to teach a lesson to Linda's students and help her plan out a future inquiry unit she was planning. To give our students a different experience, we also required them to spend time observing in their content area at Fenton High School. The demographic of Fenton is nearly the polar opposite of Flint, so Laura and I required students to reflect on specific elements in their Fenton placement. We thought this would create some excellent discussions when we were back in Flint.

As often happens with PBTE, everything does not always go to plan. Linda went on medical leave early on in our semester, and the substitute shortage in Flint meant that her class was taught by a rotation of paraprofessionals from the school. Place-based elements were nonexistent without Linda there; in fact, there wasn't much education happening at all. One day, we walked into the class to find students half-heartedly working on

Place-Based Teacher Education in Flint

assignments from their other classes while the paraprofessional was wearing headphones, watching *Grey's Anatomy* on her computer. Sometimes the conference room we met in would be locked and Laura or I would have to track down a custodian to open it for us, losing precious class time in the process. One day we never found anyone, and the secretary located an empty classroom for us that was being used as a makeshift storage unit for furniture. We did our best to put the random chairs in a circle and moved on with class. And then there were the typical school interruptions—one class was interrupted by a fire drill. Since we didn't have a lot of time left, and I really needed to go over an assignment with them, we stood outside in the snow with our handouts, conducting class in the parking lot (Figure 8.1).

We could tell that our students were frustrated and uncomfortable. Laura and I did our best to talk to the students about what they were seeing at Flint Southwestern to get them to reflect on their feelings about the school and why it might be so jarring for them to see what they were seeing. We also tried to help students tap into what they had learned about Flint and why Southwestern might be understaffed and under-resourced. But our students didn't seem to be buying what we were selling. To make matters worse, our students were making all the wrong kinds of comparisons to their placements in Fenton: about how much *more* they were seeing in their

Figure 8.1. *Teaching During a Fire Drill at Flint Southwestern High School*

Photo by Laura McLeman

placements in Fenton, how much better the school was run, how clean it was—all of this with no willingness to engage in discussion as to why this was the case. Laura and I tried to bring the focus back to the assets of Flint Southwestern. One day we took a break from Linda's class and had students observe other teachers. One science teacher had students take care of their class pet, Monty the Python. We even had them observe a Latin class! What high schools still offer Latin?

One of the benefits of having your course meet in a school is that your students get to experience and observe all aspects of teaching and learning. One of the challenges of having your course meet in a school is that your students get to experience and observe all aspects of teaching and learning—the good, the bad, and the ugly. When students are experiencing firsthand the challenges of teaching in an under-resourced urban school with the kind of storied history that Flint has had, they're seeing firsthand that it's *hard*. When they're immersed in that environment, I believe it can make it harder for some to be able to look at their experience with a critical eye. Laura and I didn't help by inadvertently setting them up to make a comparison to Fenton. Some of them went to class at Southwestern in the morning and tried to participate in a discussion in a storage room, and then in the afternoon went to a beautifully well-lighted classroom in Fenton to watch a veteran educator teach lessons in their content area. Perhaps Laura and I realized this was happening too late and didn't properly scaffold the course, or perhaps these particular students never made connections from their previous place-based courses to what they were seeing. Or maybe it was both. I know I learned a valuable lesson about immersing students in a community without proper context.

PARTNERING WITH BEECHER COMMUNITY SCHOOLS

After our experience at Flint Southwestern, Laura and I co-taught again the very next semester. This time, though, we were teaching a far different course—"Teachers, Schools, and Society." I likened this course to a place-based social foundations course. The goals of the course were to learn about contemporary and historical issues in education and how they apply or have applied locally. This course technically came before the "Seminar in Methods" course in the secondary program; the idea was that students could see the complex relationship between communities and schools in context so that when they went to a school like Flint Southwestern, they may have some more contextual background for what they would experience there. When we taught "Seminar in Methods," we erroneously assumed that students would make the connection between the courses on their own. Since we now knew better, we knew we had to be more direct and explicit, starting with this course.

Suzanne Knight had taught this course before us, and she had a good experience centering the course within a whole community, not only schools in that community. This way, students can literally see how the two entities interact. For this task, we knew we needed a community partner willing to learn alongside our students, but not just one partner. We needed an entire city. So, we turned to Beecher, Michigan. If I thought Flint had a small town feel to it, it was nothing compared to Beecher. Beecher is literally a small town that touches the boundaries of the north side of Flint. Only about five square miles, Beecher was once considered a prime destination for middle-class GM workers because of its affordable housing. It was one of the more integrated cities in the Flint area because real estate agents actually sold houses to Black families in the 1960s (Highsmith, 2012). When an influx of cheap, shoddy, public housing units went into Beecher at a disproportionate rate compared to other areas of Flint (whiter areas of Flint), home values dropped, and many residents foreclosed on their homes thanks in part to the economic crises of the 1970s. The construction and consequent abandonment of these homes caused massive blockbusting, white flight, and racial tensions over the following decades (Highsmith, 2012). At one point, Beecher had more than 15,000 residents in those five miles; in 2020, there were less than half that number (United States Census Bureau, n.d.a).

The Beecher community is closely tied to Flint due to proximity but is also a place with its own identity. The school district is small—only one elementary school and a middle/high school—but they were more than willing to partner with our entire university, not just education programs. UM-Flint set up a classroom and meeting space meant for dual use by the Beecher community and UM-Flint. Called the Neff Center, many UM-Flint classes were held there. Beecher High School students and UM-Flint students often worked side by side in a variety of fields. When the secondary redesign team wanted a school district to partner with, Beecher seemed a logical choice. They were easier to communicate with than Flint Community Schools (FCS) but had a similar demographic of students as Flint, with a similar history. Beecher staff were part of our many conversations about the secondary education program. That day at the Stockton House, we had at least three teachers and administrators from Beecher giving input on which course experiences would be necessary for our teacher candidates. Because the staff was so involved in our program development, the district became a natural partner for us. It helped to have Lance Sumpter, Beecher High School principal, develop the course objectives for the "Teachers, Schools and Society" course because he knew exactly what to do when we wanted to hold one of our class meetings at Beecher High School. He knew what to say when he spoke to our students, which teachers' classrooms to visit, what district data to show us, and how to answer our students' questions.

Maria Salinas was a Beecher alum who worked in our Center for Educator Preparation. Maria knew everyone in Beecher, and this was not an exaggeration. None of the secondary courses I taught would have been possible without Maria. She connected my students in the "Teacher and Learner" course with Beecher High School teachers for tutoring and classroom observations and opened the Neff Center for us to hold classes at BHS. For "Teachers, Schools, and Society," Maria was able to find numerous Beecher community organizations, businesses, and events that our students could attend to practice understanding how schools and communities are connected.

Because our program was developed along with Beecher educators, residents, and alumni (some people were all three!) and many of the course experiences took place there, my students really were immersed in place throughout their entire time at UM-Flint, not just in any one course. Some of their experiences were out in the community as well as in Beecher schools. For "Teachers, Schools, and Society," they attended parent meetings at the elementary school, visited the Beecher library, and attended a school board meeting. Two of my students were able to interview the superintendent. Maria even drove some of our students around in her van, giving tours of the 5 miles of Beecher, a village that many students assumed was part of Flint. Having a district partner in our program allowed students to learn from *people* outside of the university in *places* outside of the university. Laura and I hoped that our "Teachers, Schools, and Society" students would be able to look at wherever they were placed for "Seminar in Methods" or in student teaching and be able to "groundtruth" (Vélez & Solórzano, 2017) their experience, even if it was hard.

PBTE AND WATER CRISIS CONNECTIONS

In fall 2015, the secondary program launched while the state was finally recognizing that Flint residents had been drinking lead-poisoned water for 18 months. I had only just learned about the water crisis from my students during "Community, Family, Self" when we were discussing community assets and injustices. That fall, Governor Snyder ordered the water source switch back to the Detroit water system, but the real fallout was just beginning. Many of the teacher educators at UM-Flint were stymied as to how to prepare our teacher candidates for what was happening on a day-to-day basis. But what about the long-term impacts of our programs? We had just redesigned many of them—did we need to do it again? Were we in good shape with our focus on place-based education? Or did we need massive revisions? Considering the water crisis, it did feel as if many conversations needed to happen again. Suzanne Knight, the leader of the secondary "redesign" team, and other colleagues of mine wrote an article reflecting on the experience of being in teacher preparation during this time of upheaval in Flint. Appropriately subtitling the article "Building the House While We're

Living in It" (2018), my colleagues asked the question, "How do the big ideas we're studying play out or manifest in this local place?" Originally, the question was developed as an essential question for our students to ask themselves. But it became an appropriate question to ask ourselves: How does teacher preparation manifest itself in Flint during the water crisis?

In their book *Preparing Teachers for Deeper Learning* (2019), Linda Darling-Hammond and Jeannie Oakes examined teacher preparation programs across the country that successfully engage their candidates in "deeper learning," with one aspect being how these programs address issues of equity and social injustice in their communities. They write that teacher preparation programs can right educational injustices by "giving the young people who are most burdened by inequality and injustice access to outstanding teachers who can afford them learning opportunities often reserved for those in the most advantaged neighborhoods with the most privileged status" (p. 265). Most of our teacher candidates come from the Flint area—either Genesee County or the northern edge of neighboring Oakland County. After graduation, many of them stay and teach in the area, often returning to where they grew up. The water crisis was uniquely Flint, affecting only the city's water. However, we knew that students impacted by the Flint water crisis extended far beyond the city limits. Flint children may attend other schools in the area, and not all children impacted were Flint residents. Our teacher candidates would be going into areas burdened by injustice, even if those places were not in the Flint city limits. And we needed to prepare them to be outstanding.

Darling-Hammond and Oakes (2019) also describe what teacher preparation programs need to provide teacher candidates to "teach at the intersection" of deep learning and equity and social justice (p. 272). They write of teacher candidates experiencing coursework that links education to social inequality, of candidates doing field placements in schools suffering from structural inequalities, and of candidates who reflect on their own identities in society and with place. We felt confident that our SEC courses did all these things, so we doubled down on making sure our students were learning. We routinely checked in with our community partners, during curriculum mapping sessions at places like the Stockton House, or when planning specific course experiences like "Teachers, Schools, and Society" in Beecher. We didn't always nail it (e.g., the Flint Southwestern experience), but when we didn't nail it, we were determined to learn more. We traveled to place-based education conferences together, we invited our EMU colleagues to come work with us, and most importantly, we constantly talked to our students about what they were getting out of the program. Many of them felt that their SEC coursework was transformative, making them appreciative for Flint and its people (Knight et al., 2018).

Creating an effective place-based teacher preparation program committed to addressing local injustices takes more than coursework and community partners. Darling-Hammond and Oakes (2019) recommend that institutional leaders at universities make teacher preparation a top priority, with dedicated resources. Teacher preparation programs are expensive and require many people dedicated to the work of field placements, community partnerships, certification requirements, and much more. Not to mention advising, field supervision, and teaching courses. When the Center for Educator Preparation opened, the university put some money into the startup of the center. When the money ran out, administration didn't invest the same amount—and then it stopped investing all together. The Neff Center, which was so highly regarded as a community and university partnership with Beecher Schools, also lost funding. At a time when UM-Flint should have been investing in teacher preparation, it was doing the exact opposite.

Over the years from the water crisis to the pandemic, enrollment at UM-Flint declined steadily. This drop in enrollment made for constant change in university administration: In nine years, there were three university chancellors, four provosts, and a rotation of vice-provosts and vice-chancellors. As we saw with FCS in Chapter 3, unstable leadership is an enemy to good place-based education. Each new person brings new priorities, new initiatives, and you must restart the process of building community relationships. On top of this, there was a national teacher shortage exacerbated by the COVID-19 pandemic. But even before then, Governor Snyder had done his best to chip away at public education in Michigan, destroying unions in the state with Right to Work laws, freezing salaries, and instituting increasingly difficult obstacles for people to earn their teacher certificate from "traditional" teacher preparation programs.

Despite how connected we were to place and community, we didn't adapt well enough to the obstacles in our path. We focused more on the students we had as opposed to trying to recruit new students. When there was no institutional support for recruiting education students, we just didn't do it. The lack of good leadership in the Education Department also kept the Center for Educator Preparation from succeeding, as turf wars over tuition (money) and governance (power) strained, and sometimes stifled, collaboration. When we should have been embracing one another, the secondary and elementary programs at times competed instead. Although we were great at focusing on place within the curriculum, we didn't always turn the lens on ourselves and adapt to what was happening at the state and national levels in teacher preparation.

LEARNING FROM FLINT: LITERALLY

A benefit in being at a smaller university is that I got to see the ins and outs of teacher preparation. Filling several roles, I learned the intricacies of how to make and keep student teaching placements, how to get students certified through the Michigan Department of Education, how to advise students through a program, how to get accreditation renewal (nationally and at the state level), and how to literally enter courses into the registration system. One of the negatives of working at a small university is that you get to see how the sausage is made—how arbitrary some systems are, how high-pressure it is working with students' graduation progress, and how frustrating it can be when the support you need from administration to prepare teachers and prepare them well just isn't there. I can't give many recommendations on how to run a place-based teacher preparation program (despite knowing a lot of the little details) because any successful place-based educational endeavor is so heavily contextualized. Sure, little details can be the same from place to place, but the big picture is always different.

It is necessary to learn about place. Not only is it important for our teacher candidates to know how to learn from a place where they may eventually end up teaching (whether it's Flint or somewhere else), teacher educators need to engage in this journey as well. The secondary education team understood this quite well. We met with community partners all over the city, and I learned a lot by exposing myself to areas of Flint through these meetings. I literally learned the geography of the city as I drove through neighborhoods, I learned history from people like Jacquie who gave me the tour of the Stockton House, and I learned about local business economies from meeting at locally owned restaurants and coffee shops like Café Rhema and the Lunch Studio. Here are some other ways I learned about teacher education and PBTE from Flint and how other teacher educators might learn about the places where they teach:

- Walk the walk, literally. Any opportunity I had to walk through neighborhoods and areas of Flint, I took. I even joined a running group while training for the Crim road race because I got the chance to explore other places. When I couldn't walk, I drove through areas of the city. Sometimes I took new routes to and from work just to explore, or I tried a different coffee shop outside of my usual haunts. (Flint has excellent coffee!)
- Go to events and programs happening in a place—for fun and for learning. I joined the Flint Community Read, where people in the city choose a book to read together each fall, meeting in various places around Flint to chat about the book each month. I also took my family to events in the city for fun—a winter carnival in Buckham Alley, shows at the Whiting, or an Inclusive Halloween event. This connected me with residents and families and gave me a new perspective on the city to enjoy it when I wasn't "working."
- Stay connected! To find out about events and programs like this, I followed community groups from Flint on Facebook, Twitter, and Instagram. I set up Google Alerts and MLive notifications

for the water crisis and for events in Flint so I wouldn't be caught unaware of what was happening in the city and new developments that might impact how I interact with my preservice teachers and community partners. I subscribed to local media like the Flintbeat and Flintside online publications so I could read media from local writers.
- Be open to learning. In addition to learning from the city and its people, I also learned quite a bit about PBTE from colleagues outside of social studies. My secondary education colleagues were from a variety of disciplines, so I got to learn about what place-based education might look like in a math class or an art class. I also learned an incredible amount from my early childhood colleagues about the place-based roots of Reggio Emilia and early childhood access. All of this learning inspired many of the chapters in this book.

Knight and colleagues (2018) wrote that we must be willing to acknowledge that in a university setting there are other teacher educators beyond those who hold the title. Community members, mentor teachers, Flint residents—all those our students connect with on their learning journey to becoming a teacher are teacher educators. We also need to be willing to relinquish the power that we hold as official teacher educators and not presume that we hold all the knowledge. Teacher educators need not even be human—the more-than-human spirit of a city is a powerful educational tool (Nxumalo, 2019).

CHAPTER 9

Place-Based Social Studies Methods in Flint

"Wait, what?!"

"There was an amusement park *here*? Like, on campus?"

My elementary social studies students were roaming the room during our final presentations of our "Right Under Our Noses" projects. On this day, students were showing off what they learned from exploring various historical sites or significant places in Flint. Half the class were standing next to posters displaying various places around the city. Well, everyone except one student was standing next to places that *currently* existed. Victor had decided to do his project on an iconic Flint place that hasn't existed since 1994 but is still a part of the local lexicon—AutoWorld. Several students gathered around Victor's poster, which featured archival photos, quotes from Flint residents about the city in the 1980s, and maps and descriptions of the location of where this Six Flags amusement park once stood—the location that is now a building on campus across the Flint River.

Although Victor had tweaked my assignment slightly, he had engaged in a historical inquiry of an important place in not just the city's history, but in the history of the University of Michigan-Flint's campus itself. AutoWorld was a massive, indoor amusement park that celebrated Flint's history and the history of the automobile. The intention of the park was to draw tourism to Flint, and it was initially successful. However, AutoWorld failed to draw the tourists it promised to, and Flint residents who visited once weren't all that interested in making repeat visits. AutoWorld existed for only six months in 1984 and has become symbolic of the economic decline and the decline of General Motors and the auto industry in Flint (Highsmith, 2015). In 1994, the park was fully demolished, and the land was given to UM-Flint, who constructed the William S. White classroom building on the riverfront site in 2002.

Since my students weren't alive in the 1980s or 1990s, and barely remember the early 2000s, the story of AutoWorld wasn't well known to them. However, it would be to their parents, and that's the generation who Victor interviewed for this project. As they read and listened to Victor's research into this particular chapter of Flint's story, some of them looked out the window toward the Flint River, perhaps imagining AutoWorld on that site. In our discussion later, where I shared what I had learned about what AutoWorld signified, many of them were amazed and encouraged to learn more about the now-historical era of the 1980s, and how their parents experienced Flint during this time. I hope many of them did ask their parents about AutoWorld, and perhaps made an intergenerational connection to that space the next time they attended class in the White Building.

I am a teacher educator who specializes in elementary social studies teacher education. I have taught a variation on the elementary social studies methods course at three different universities for the last 12 years. When I started teaching social studies methods in graduate school at Michigan State University, I had just come from working at NHA, where any professional development I presented had to apply to teachers across the country. In many ways, I approached teaching social studies methods the same way. I taught about instructional practices, social studies content, and critical issues without ever mentioning the Lansing area, where my students were actually in schools every week in a field placement. It wasn't until I started teaching social studies methods in Flint that I understood that my teaching had to adapt to place. This chapter describes a bit of that journey, which is still evolving, and what my students and I learned along the way. In this chapter, all names of my students are pseudonyms.

PLACE-BASED SOCIAL STUDIES METHODS

As mentioned in previous chapters, place-based education has a natural fit within the field of social studies. "Place" is one of the five themes of geography, involving a study of the characteristics of locations (Gersmehl, 2014). But place is also about many subjective qualities, such as how individuals feel about a place—nostalgia and discomfort alike. Place is about how the culture of a physical space transforms individuals and builds connections and relationships, such as how residents attach meaning to spaces and power to authority figures, as two examples (Resor, 2010). The subjectivity of the concept of a "sense of place" (Resor, 2010, p. 186) can lead to great inquiry questions, leading students to investigate their own communities, how they interact with their communities, and how they are shaped by their communities.

Connecting social studies content to students' real lives is one aspect of place-based education. Maguth and Hilburn (2011) wrote a lesson where they refer to their communities in Ohio as "learning laboratories" (p. 27) where students study a local industry and the historical, economic, political, social, environmental, and technological connections to the area. Resor (2010) describes partnering with a local museum to develop a map or a historical "quest" of the community to develop a historical tour for visitors. Although connecting content to the real world is a good start, in the critical tradition of social studies, students can push their study of place even further, viewing the subjective elements of place through a lens of identity and social justice. Gruenewald (2003b) describes the connection of critical pedagogy to a pedagogy of place because places also represent injustices and shape social institutions (Kitchens, 2009). Inquiry in social studies can be a natural place for students to examine why some people might feel at home in a place and others don't, or why some people are allowed to move through a space freely and others can't. The concept of civic action, or taking informed action (NCSS, 2013) is important to the social studies field as well. Developing a connection to community can lead students to want to be more civically engaged, and when the community is used as a learning space it can facilitate this connection (Seneschal, 2007).

With the many connections that place-based education has in the field of social studies, there isn't as much research on place-based education in social studies methods courses. In the last chapter, I described some of the literature about place-based teacher education (PBTE) more broadly, and in Michigan specifically with the Great Lakes Stewardship Initiative (GLSI). And certainly, the literature on K–12 students understanding their communities, engaging in learning with community partners and residents, and reflecting on their identity could also apply to preservice teachers. In 2007, Todd and Brinkman published their work with a local museum's education outreach program as a field experience for teacher candidates in a summer social studies methods course. Their main goal was to give the preservice teachers the opportunity to display competencies for their program in lieu of a traditional student teaching experience. Almost as tangential benefits, the article mentions that teachers developed into more active citizens and the museum found the partnership enriching.

Recent research into place-based social studies methods pushes further into a more critical pedagogy of place. Thacker and Bodle (2022) used a place-based social studies methods course to advance their teacher candidates' racial literacies. The course took place in the community at a site of racial trauma—Montpelier, the James Madison plantation in Virginia—and required students to rethink their relationship with this space through reflection. Involving teacher candidates in addressing community issues or engaging in deep reflection at a community site is the opposite of "guerrilla teaching," as described by Zygmunt and Clark (2016). It's more of a methodical, slow, process of deeper learning. Popielarz and Galliher (2023) described a community-based social studies methods course centered on the city of Detroit. The students in this course learned social studies content through multimodal texts, including a documentary about the city, guest speakers by local journalists and historians, and a tour of the local library. They applied their learning by designing a journey box featuring counter-narratives in Detroit and wrote a lesson plan around an asset map of a Detroit neighborhood. Through reflective journals, the teacher candidates found themselves "(re)learning" social studies and, for some, learning more about Detroit along the way.

Place-based teacher preparation has a natural fit in social studies teacher preparation. As mentioned in Chapter 8, I found a deep connection to my colleagues in other disciplines at UM-Flint in their desire to create a place-based secondary education program. But developing into a place-based social studies teacher educator is a journey—one that the water crisis accelerated for me.

ELEMENTARY SOCIAL STUDIES METHODS IN FLINT

It's important to understand the context in which my students in Flint were learning to be teachers. The University of Michigan-Flint is a 4-year university located in downtown Flint on the banks of the Flint River. UM-Flint is not an extension of the larger University of Michigan campus in Ann Arbor. The "-Flint" marks significant differences. Students don't take classes in both places, and the universities (along with UM-Dearborn) are separate in many ways. UM-Flint is significantly smaller (only 4,500 undergraduates in 2021 compared to the 32,000 in Ann Arbor [*U.S. News and World Report*, 2023]), cheaper to attend (Michigan Senate Fiscal Agency [MISFA], n.d.), and less selective—UM-Flint accepts roughly 66% of their applicants, compared to 20% in Ann Arbor (Jordan, 2021; University of Michigan-Flint, 2023). However, the campuses are very much connected, for better or for worse. For example, although UM-Flint has its own chancellor and cabinet, the UM-Flint chancellor reports to the president of the University of Michigan, essentially making the Flint and Dearborn campuses on a lower tier compared to the Ann Arbor campus.

One major difference between the Ann Arbor and Flint campuses is that UM-Flint was, and still is, considered mostly a "commuter school." UM-Flint has residence halls, but most of the students come into the city from outlying areas to go to school, often coming back for second degrees or degrees later in life. Being a commuter school means that most of my students only came into the city for classes, and then immediately left. In the 1980s, the university encouraged this by installing skyways over Flint city streets connecting campus buildings. These enclosed glass skyways, called the "hamster tunnels," meant that students literally never had to step foot in the city of Flint (Highsmith, 2015). In fact, the entrance to the campus library is accessible only through one of these skyways—there is no public-facing entrance.

UM-Flint has a slightly more racially and ethnically diverse population than the campus in Ann Arbor, but probably not as diverse as one would think. One could assume that UM-Flint would mirror the city of Flint when it came to race and ethnic diversity, but it does not. For example, although nearly 57% of the city's population identify as Black, only 12% of UM-Flint students did so in the fall of 2022 (United States Census Bureau, n.d.b; University of Michigan-Flint, 2023). The teaching profession in the United States is made up of primarily white women—nearly 80% (NCES, n.d.), and in this category, UM-Flint was closer to the national statistics. Although UM-Flint doesn't keep records of race and gender by program, the School of Education and Human Services (which included education and social work programs) was made up of 75% white students and 81% female students (University of Michigan-Flint, 2023). The fact that my students were mostly white women who came into Flint only to go to class meant that I often had to deal with biases and stereotypes about the city and its residents that stemmed from lack of exposure to the area and a narrative of Flint as a violent place. At the minimum, most of my students knew very little about Flint, despite coming to the city multiple times a week. This was illustrated for me quite clearly in my elementary social studies methods course in early 2016.

In 2016, elementary education students took one social studies methods course in their program, and since the program was so small, only one section was offered each semester (and then eventually only once a year), and it was always taught by me. I was the only social studies teacher educator at the entire university. Although there wasn't a definitive sequence for when the students had to take my methods course, the students had to take the class before their extensive field placements for their pre–student teaching and their student teaching semesters. This meant that my students were not regularly in classrooms while taking the course and were somewhere in the middle of their teacher preparation experience. When the water crisis hit and became well known around the world, my first inclination was to check on my students' well-being. I asked them often how they were doing, how they felt about the national attention, how they felt about being exposed to lead on campus. They mostly gave me surface answers, which wasn't unusual. I was just happy to hold space for them if they needed it. But then I began to make connections to our social studies content and the water crisis as it was happening. I would often pull news items that had just come up and weave that into our topic. For example, when we discussed compelling questions, I used the example, "Should people have to pay for water?" because news of Flint residents refusing to pay their water bills in protest was a major headline. On a day when I planned to talk about teaching civics and government to elementary students, I used several examples of local activists exposing the water crisis to discuss community action.

My attempts at weaving what the students were experiencing into the content of the course was met with . . . crickets. Sometimes I could see their body language changing when I brought up the water crisis in class. They would slump over, turn to their laptops, and tune me out completely. I was baffled by this response. At this same time, I was also teaching the student teaching seminar and the pre–student teaching seminar course. My students in those classes were near the end of their elementary education program and spending most of their time in schools in Flint. To compare these courses to my social studies methods course, my students in the field-heavy courses wanted to discuss the water crisis frequently. My students at Freeman Elementary (like Hana from Chapter 2) wanted more information—what signs to look for in their students that they might be exposed to lead, for example. When I checked on their well-being, they were honest; since they had also been exposed to lead on campus and in their placements, they wanted to talk about their concerns and fears about their own health and the health of their own children.

So why wouldn't the social studies class engage in the same way? I began to see my social studies education colleagues post resources on social media along the lines of "how to teach about the Flint water crisis" or a "Flint syllabus" and I would feel something like annoyance, but it was probably more like jealousy. How easy must it be to be able to integrate what was happening in Flint into social studies instruction from a distance. Up close, it wasn't remotely easy. Finally, after one of my discussion questions was met with literal silence, I broke down and asked my social studies methods students why they didn't want to talk about the water crisis. One student told me, "We just hear about it so much. It's everywhere. I just want to come to class and not have to think about it."

I thought so much about that statement in the days, weeks, and years afterward. On one hand, it was a trauma response. Whether my students were from Flint or not, they were victims of the water crisis. If they lived in Flint, they were still showering with water bottles and trying to get access to filters. If they didn't live in Flint, they might have been drinking the water on campus. All of them knew what it was like to have the spotlight on them and to be seen as a victim. I resonated with the idea that they might want one space in their life where they didn't have to focus on their trauma. On the other hand, I looked at that statement as a failure on my part to have my classroom be truly part of the community, part of the city. Because if it was, the water crisis wouldn't be seen as an "extra" topic that their professor kept bringing up but part of the history of a place that forms who we were and how we looked at the world. I think my field-heavy courses embraced this more because the students were actually out in the city more often. They were eager to talk about and process their experiences as a result. Learning to teach in Flint made them open to being transformed by that place. Since my social studies methods course didn't have a field placement in a school, and wouldn't have one for the foreseeable future, I knew I had to do better about making the city my social studies "field placement." And it went beyond just using local examples in my regularly scheduled syllabus.

In the semesters following, I did a complete overhaul of my elementary social studies methods course directly because of the water crisis. I turned my methods courses completely into an examination of place. Of Flint. The course developed from "How do we teach elementary social studies?" to "How do we teach elementary social studies in Flint?" Once that overarching question for my course changed, the content had to change. My students needed to know more about Flint. The following sections describe how I went from taking my students on field trips to asking them to do deep inquiries into the city and to examine its spatial injustices.

FIELD TRIPS

As mentioned before, many of my students came to Flint only for class and then immediately left. If they had class all day, they would stay on campus, eating in our University Center and napping on large benches outside my office, as college students often do. My students could park their car, attend class, eat, nap, and go home all without once stepping into the city of Flint. Depending on where they parked, they might not even need to spend any time outdoors thanks to the "hamster tunnel" skyways. Gruenewald (2003a) believed this kind of isolated education "limits[s] experience and perception" and "potentially stunt[s] human development" (p. 625) because students are not able to understand how their school/education is intertwined with community (Kitchens, 2009). It's the difference between investing very little in a community as a temporary resident versus the knowledge, care, and rootedness of an "inhabitant" (Gruenewald, 2003b; Orr, 1994). Kitchens calls the former a "pedagogy of placelessness" (2009, p. 255).

I believed that my students' "placelessness" regarding Flint hindered their abilities to understand social studies teaching, as well as their abilities to be good teachers. A bold statement, perhaps, but I also believed it was my responsibility to teach them to be good inhabitants of the city. For me, this started with getting them out there. Since I knew they might not do this on their own, I needed to make getting out into the city part of my course. I also knew that many of my students were nervous about the city, thanks to the dominant narrative of Flint as a violent place. I decided to start simple: the Flint Farmers' Market.

Flint Farmers' Market

The Flint Farmers' Market moved to a site one block from my office downtown in 2014. It's a massive indoor/outdoor market open three days a week, year-round. There are many food vendors from various cultures; there's fresh produce, coffee, shops, and meeting spaces. It is one of the rare places in Flint where one can buy fresh food. Shortly after the water crisis hit, Dr. Mona put a health clinic inside the building as well. The market is constantly bustling with people. Since it is literally a one-minute walk from campus, I started taking my students there to look for the "social studies" at the market. We would walk over together as a class, and I would let them loose, telling them to take pictures (in the style of photovoice methodology [Latz, 2017]) of what they found to be representative of any social studies disciplines and concepts. We took our time with this, and I encouraged them to buy some food, window shop, or sit and observe for a bit. Then we would walk back to our classroom together and share our pictures, students excitedly noticing things in each other's photos that they had missed. I could then lead into a conversation about why the market is located where it is, the economically motivated debates during the planning stages, and what the market means to the community.

Walking Downtown

After a couple of semesters of Farmers' Market trips, I decided to up my game a little and take my classes on a walk through a few blocks downtown. I was teaching them now about the five themes of geography, and I thought about how much we could see related to geography content just by walking around—not just where things were located but the culture of a place, how people interact with the environment, the movement of people and things, and how areas of the city are classified into regions. The first time I did this, I asked my friend Tom, a professor in the History Department, to come with us. He specialized in local Flint history and had done a lot of place-based work in his classes, as he does quite a bit of public historical work. I knew he would be able to fill in gaps in my historical knowledge. With Tom on board, I got excited about our first neighborhood walk.

I told my students a week before that we would be going on the walk and to dress appropriately and wear comfortable shoes. Quite frankly, they looked horrified. That semester, I taught the course as an evening class, and it was November in Michigan. This meant that walking around 6 p.m. would be dark and cold. I addressed their concerns by saying that I walked downtown after dark many times (which was true), and I felt no less safe than I did in any other place (which was true). They seemed unconvinced. However, when Tom showed up, he had his dog Buck with him, and the vibe instantly changed. Although it was still dark and cold, the group learned a lot from Tom and me. They were constantly taking pictures and talking of how beautiful the city was lit up at night. (See Figure 9.1.) And we got to have a conversation about their initial perceptions and feelings, as well as their new understandings. It's the first and perhaps only time that a dog made a significant difference in my teaching (thanks, Buck).

We went on many more walks in many more semesters, each time planning them a little differently. I made sure to do this earlier in the semester, so the weather and daylight was in our favor, and I incorporated some of what I learned from Tom on that first tour, so he didn't need to accompany us every time. In 2019, the Flint Public Art Project had literally hundreds of

Place-Based Social Studies Methods in Flint   129

Figure 9.1. *My Students, Dr. Henthorn, and Buck*

murals painted around the city, many of them downtown. New murals were popping up everywhere, so I started making the murals key points of our walking tour so we could talk about how place influences art, and vice versa. Each student group became less nervous about walking around downtown, even as I regularly made back alleys and parking lots part of our tour because they were covered in beautiful art.

Haunted Houses and Local Businesses

We soon began spending entire class periods off campus. Although I did this quite often when I taught other classes in the secondary program (see Chapter 8), I hadn't done it as much with social studies methods courses. Part of the reason was that the Education Department didn't have as many systems in place for partnering with the community as my secondary education colleagues had. For a while these courses were separate for me until I started using resources I learned from teaching my secondary education coursework into social studies methods. Our University Outreach office put me in touch with the Whaley House, a historical museum created out of an old Flint family home within walking distance of campus. Samantha, the director at the time, was trying to put together an elementary education program for local field trips, so we had her practice with us. My students looked at artifacts, toured the home, and discussed historical thinking for elementary students. Another semester, we toured the home looking for examples of "cultural universals" (Brophy & Alleman, 2006) that we could use to design inquiry questions around.

I also spent a class at the Stockton House. Jacquie took my students on the same tour she gave me when I first visited with the secondary education group. Just as I had, my students asked if the place was haunted, and just as she had said to me, Jacquie confirmed her belief in the presence of friendly ghosts in the building. My students were clearly fascinated by this idea, so Jacquie took them to the lower depths of the house, showing them the morgue and embalming rooms from when the house was a hospital. Jacquie expertly adapted her instruction based on what students were interested in and used her same questioning, although I admit that after *that* tour, my students were not as interested in debriefing Jacquie's teaching techniques as they were discussing the various supernatural presences they were *sure* they felt in the embalming room.

When we studied economic concepts, I took my methods students to two local businesses downtown located across from each other on the same street: Comma Bookstore and the Reclaimed by Whaley clothing store. The two managers of the stores were eager to talk about how they work together and collaborate with each other rather than compete. We visited the Ferris Wheel Building, which serves as a hub for local entrepreneurs to develop business ideas. The group 100K Ideas offers guidance for people wanting to start businesses in Flint and connects them to local microfinancing. We had great discussions about the different kind of community capitalism happening downtown and the significance of minority-owned businesses lifting each other up.

This was all content we could have learned in the classroom, but now my students got to see it applied in the city. Not only do I believe their learning was strengthened, but my teaching was as well. Having people like Tom, Jacquie, Samantha, and the local business owners teaching all or parts of my courses gave me new ideas and inspiration. But most important, I believe these field trips helped my students see a new counternarrative of Flint (Butler & Sinclair, 2020), one where despite the city being marginalized for decades, people of Flint have created spaces of beauty and prosperity—"geographies of hope" (Yosso et al., 2009, p. 677). Art, commerce, history, and culture have always been ever-present in the city, and I know the field trips we took exposed my students to some of that, which many of them had not seen before. On my course evaluations, there is always one question regarding how the course could be improved. Inevitably, someone writes "more field trips." Every single time.

RIGHT UNDER OUR NOSES

For a final in my social studies methods course, I used to have my students create a social studies lesson plan. At first, the lesson had to be based on a "big idea," but then as I tried to incorporate more of NCSS's C3 Framework (2013) into my courses, they had to create lessons around compelling questions. No matter what my students called it, they struggled with lesson planning as seeing a lesson as a part of a whole, a sustained inquiry. Eventually, I realized that perhaps allowing them to engage in a sustained inquiry as a student would help them see how one could look in a classroom. I created an inquiry around the compelling question, "What makes Flint special?" This question mirrors some of the language in the 2nd- and 3rd-grade Michigan social studies standards about studying the local community and the unique features of our state. I then told students they would be visiting places in the city, learning what they could about these places, and then teaching it back to us. Our final assignment was for my students to "answer" the compelling question of what makes Flint special from the evidence they learned from their inquiry and their classmates' inquiries. We still did lesson plans, but now my students had something to draw on.

This assignment was taken from Katy Swalwell, a Lead Equity Specialist from the Equity Literacy Institute. When Katy was a social studies teacher educator at the University of Wisconsin-Madison, she took her class on the First Nations Cultural Landscape Tour, led by Aaron Bird Bear, an Indigenous scholar and citizen of the Mandan, Hidatsa, and Diné nations. Bird Bear created the tour to introduce students to the First Nations of Wisconsin (Erikson, 2022). Katy's class was one of many to take the tour over the course of several years, and she found it inspirational. Her students were looking with new eyes at places they had passed many times, seeing these places through a lens of spatial justice and equity. She created an assignment where her students would have to explore other places like this in their community and teach it to others. She called it "Right Under Our Noses" (Rodríguez & Swalwell, 2021).

I adapted the assignment slightly by adding the compelling question and narrowing my students' choices. They had two options—they could research and learn about well-known public sites in the city (preferably historical sites) or map a place in the city that had meaning to them. My rules were that they either had to visit their site or had been to at least a part of the area they were mapping, and they needed to include photo evidence. They presented their projects during our final class in any form they liked (poster, brochure, video, etc.), and after that class, they wrote a reflection about what makes Flint special, including what they learned from themselves and others. The first time I did this assignment, I was blown away by what my students had learned, how excited they were to share and learn from others, and their level of engagement with the city.

Brienne and the Waterfall

Brienne chose to visit Steppingstone Falls, a park surrounding a waterfall on the north end of the city. She lived near this area and had seen the signs for the park, which made her choose to explore this place for the assignment. She took several photos on the waterfall itself, one of them at daybreak, which she took before going to class one morning. In her presentation, she frequently referenced the beauty of the waterfall in the morning light, describing how she visited there multiple times for this assignment to take photos in a different light. Beauty was a common theme for Brienne, even referencing that the point of the assignment was to find the "beauty" in the city, which although a lovely side effect of the assignment wasn't its explicit purpose.

Brienne posted her photos to her personal public Instagram (not a requirement of the project), and when I asked her why, she described wanting to show other people the beauty in Flint:

> I thought it would be fun to let other people know that this is part of Flint . . . I never knew it was a thing and I found out it was really pretty . . . Another reason I posted it on Instagram was because Flint gets such a bad rap. Flint is actually really beautiful. You just have to explore it a little deeper, I guess.

Brienne expressed genuine surprise at seeing this natural phenomenon in an urban center and spoke of enlightening others on what she found, perhaps expecting that others wouldn't expect to see Steppingstone Falls in Flint, either. In her reflection paper, she referenced the fact that people in other countries knew of Flint because of the high crime rate and other issues. She wrote: "If we change the way we see things, we change the way we talk about them."

Willow and the Factory

Willow chose to visit Factory Two, an old carriage factory that had been recently restored as a historical site downtown. Willow chose this place because she could see the factory from her dorm, and she had walked past it on her way home and wondered if it had historical significance. The research Willow completed for this assignment was extensive—she took numerous photos of the structure and was eager to share everything she learned about the history of the factory and its significance to the city as she talked through each photo individually.

Like Brienne, Willow expressed surprise that the factory (which she had originally thought was an abandoned building) was a historic site not only relevant to Flint but to United States' history as well.

> I didn't grow up in Flint; I'm an hour away. I didn't know [the history] . . . No one would ever know what [the factory] was unless they were purposefully researching something . . . which kind of shows the blindness to the things around us when we're tunneling in on things.

Willow's experience learning so much history about what she thought was an ordinary brick building changed how she approached looking at other structures in the city. "If things like [the factory] can get historic site markers . . . what else could?"

Unique Deviations

As with any good inquiry, some students found themselves going on tangential explorations based on what they found, which also led to some amazing experiences. Two students visited the Sloan Museum and were so inspired by the exhibit on redlining there that they shared their project on redlining in Flint as opposed to the Sloan Museum as a place. One student researched the history of the Vernors mural on the site of an old building downtown. Before the Flint Public Art Project, this was the original downtown art! In her quest, she discovered the many different places this one building had been over the years, including a sandwich shop—hence the reason for a giant Vernors ad, which was now vintage. I used information she found on my downtown tours in semesters to come. And the story at the top of this chapter was about Victor, who chose to share a place that no longer existed. And although he couldn't take a selfie of himself at AutoWorld, he shared numerous historical photos along with interviews from his family members who did remember the old amusement park.

All these students either spoke or wrote about their perceptions of Flint changing because of getting out in the community to explore a specific location. Their changing perspectives are evidence of the disruption of their preconceived notions about Flint, and the first step in placemaking (Demarest, 2015)—rethinking what they know about *where* they're learning.

TEACHING CRITICAL GEOGRAPHY

Once I started getting my students out into the city more, I found it easier to engage them in critical topics related to spatial injustice in Flint. After visiting the Farmers' Market and seeing how many people relied on the market for food, it was easier to talk about its role in helping Flint become less of a food desert. After a tour of downtown and taking pictures next to a Flint sign in a grassy space, we could discuss how that space was once an office building called Genesee Towers. We could discuss why Genesee Towers was imploded to add more green space in the city and who benefits and who doesn't benefit from that decision. Having specific experiences to draw on helped my students make connections to more critical topics, rather than me bringing them up and hoping they would make connections on their own.

In addition to providing necessary context for my students, getting out in the city also inspired them to take up other critical topics on their own. One example is when Britt visited the Flint Sit-Down Strike memorial. Britt was from the Detroit area, so she admitted she knew virtually nothing about Flint, let alone anything about the Sit-Down Strike. The Sit-Down Strike is considered one of the most influential events of the labor movement to date. Over the course of 44 days, GM workers barricaded themselves inside the Fisher Body Plant in Flint to strike against low wages, poor working conditions, and the fact that GM bosses were firing any workers who expressed interest in joining the United Auto Workers (UAW) union. At the time, the concept of a sit-down strike was revolutionary as it kept GM from sending in replacement workers, making it more difficult for them to ignore the demands (Loomis, 2018).

After visiting the monument, Britt was moved by one part of the memorial that depicts a policeman dragging a woman away by her collar. Britt focused her presentation on the Flint Women's Auxiliary, a group of women who supported the men inside the Fisher Plant during the strike by providing them supplies, picketing outside the building, and even acting as human shields from police provocations (Loomis, 2018). The class was fascinated by these women, and we talked about why their contribution to the Flint Sit-Down Strike might be lesser known outside of Flint, as well as the sexism many of the women experienced trying to contribute to the movement.

Our trip to the Farmers' Market and conversations about Flint as a food desert had inspired Renee to plot where Flint's food sources were—grocery stores, convenience stores, and liquor stores. In that same class, Sarah had chosen to plot out the locations of all the schools that had been closed in the city. That semester, I had students do a gallery walk with their final projects, where half the class set up stations like a conference poster session and the other half walked around engaging the presenters in informal conversations about what they had learned. At one point, I watched Sarah carry her map over to Renee's station, so I joined their conversation. They were comparing each other's maps of closed schools and lack of access to food and noticed a significant amount of overlap. With the two of them, we discussed how these phenomena could be related and how systemic racism plays a part in the under-resourcing of communities. The use of GIS technology could have made these connections easier for the students to make, but Renee and Sarah showed that using GIS isn't completely necessary for students to get the general idea of spatial injustices in their community. They were able to "ground-truth" some of the topics we had discussed in class and teach each other about what they found (Vélez & Solórzano, 2017).

LEARNING FROM FLINT: TRANSFORMING INTO PLACE-BASED TEACHERS

Soja (2010) wrote that we are all "intrinsically spatial beings from birth, we are at all times engaged and enmeshed in shaping our socialized spatialities and, simultaneously, being shaped by them" (p. 18). I think that many preservice teachers understand that they go into a classroom with the intention of shaping young minds. I know I have had many preservice teachers who have seen teaching as a world-changing profession, with the ability to make their communities better places by sending out educated children into the world. I don't disagree that these are worthwhile goals. Certainly, an under-resourced area such as Flint, which has experienced injustice at deadly levels, deserves the best teachers. Teachers who believe in improving the city through educating its children. What I don't think my teacher candidates understood, initially, was how much the city of Flint—and by extension, its history, culture, and people—would and could shape *them*. When they're experiencing Flint as just a place where they drop in a few times a week to attend school, they don't have the opportunity to be shaped by the city at all. They have to be open to the notion of reciprocity that Soja describes, but they don't know what they don't know.

Below are some ways that I pushed the issue and made my students get to know Flint and reflect on how the city has shaped them and education within it. My goal is that even if these students don't end up teaching in Flint, they will take the practice and process of understanding place wherever they go (Noddings, 2002). Teacher educators could do the same.

- First, students need to physically get out of the classroom. I will be the first to claim that when we took walks of the city, our limited time and our location allowed us to walk through only the downtown and Cultural Center neighborhoods. These neighborhoods have different histories and resources than others in Flint, so sometimes taking a "windshield tour" is necessary. I mentioned in Chapter 8 that Maria, our CEP staff, would take students on tours in her van. If you can, find a Maria! Rodríguez and Swalwell (2021) also recommend taking a "algorithmic walk," where you take a somewhat arbitrary walking route to see where you end up (two blocks right, then three blocks left, etc.).
- When your students are out in a place, encourage them to interact as they normally would and not be in "learning mode" all the time. When we went to the Farmers' Market, I encouraged them to get lunch or a snack, and we took some time to sit and eat there. When we went to local businesses, we took time to browse and window shop after presentations from the owners, with some students choosing to purchase things. Not only is this putting money back into the local businesses, but it's likely to encourage repeat visits or further exploration.
- Be mindful of students' perceptions of "safety" in a place and meet them where they are. Most of my white female students were afraid to walk the city at night and certainly felt better with Tom and

his dog accompanying us. Students of color may not feel safe in certain environments where people are predominantly white. Addressing students' feelings as real, while encouraging them to experience places regardless of their feelings, is a tough balance. I have worked with some students one on one who expressed severe reservations about visiting certain places, and I had to try to find ways to make them more comfortable.
- Whenever possible, I combine the physical act of getting out into a place with bringing up issues of spatial injustices we see along the way. Butler and Sinclair (2020) call for researchers to better understand how inequality is contained in and shapes places through conducting place inquiries. The Right Under Our Noses projects turn my students into critical place researchers, and with guidance they're able to understand connections.

In the spirit of reciprocity, I should mention how much my preservice teachers over the years have taught me. If it wasn't for my social studies methods students rejecting my methods in early 2016, I might not have been motivated to overhaul my course as critically place-based. Many Right Under Our Noses projects have inspired me to visit certain places in Flint that I hadn't been to but I'd learned about from my students. Willow's trip to Factory Two in particular inspired me to go on a walk in the Carriage Town neighborhood where Factory Two is located, reading the historical markers. Other students' research inspired me to add more to future semesters about topics such as redlining, the history of Saginaw Street businesses, and the Flint Women's Auxiliary. Also important, taking students into the city brought me a renewed sense of joy. In addition to getting to spend more time outdoors and away from screens, I truly loved watching my students fall in love with Flint. Seeing the city through their eyes made me fall in love with the city (and teaching) over and over again.

Part IV

WHERE DO WE GO FROM HERE?

CHAPTER 10

What I Learned From Flint

It's 6 o'clock in the morning, and I'm sitting on the edge of my hotel room bed searching my phone for a convenience store or something open at that early hour. I'm at a conference in San Diego and forgot to fill my water bottle at the convention center, or to buy a new one the day before. I'm thirsty and want to make coffee, but no luck—nothing is open. I look through the open bathroom door and think, *you have running water right here. Just use that.* But that thought exits my brain as quickly as it entered. I am staying at an older hotel. Drinking tap water is not an option. Since this older hotel also has no gift shop, vending machine, or snack area from which to get water, I contemplate asking the front desk employees if they have a fridge with bottled water somewhere in the back. *That's ridiculous*, I think. *Just use the bathroom sink.* But I can't make myself do it. I Google, "Is the water in San Diego safe to drink?" and drop down a rabbit hole of lead-testing reports, searching for California's Lead & Copper Rule threshold. At one point, I stop to contemplate the craziness of my situation. Out of force of habit, I have spent several minutes searching for water when perfectly safe water is right in front of me.

This was not the first time I had done this since 2014. Wherever I was, If I didn't have access to filtered water, I would simply go thirsty rather than drink out of a tap. And that's exactly what I did that early morning in San Diego.

Periodically, people will ask me the question I mentioned in the introduction of this book: "Is the water crisis over?" I never quite know how to answer. I think the crisis is improving. More homes have filtered water, more pipes are being replaced, Michigan's lead-testing threshold is strict, and younger kids are trusting the filters more at school. But, no doubt, there are many people like me who distrust tap water anywhere. We also know for a fact that there are children in Flint who will be living with the water crisis forever as they navigate possible academic and social difficulties from lead poisoning. And Flint teachers will have the impact of the water crisis looming over them for years to come as they educate these children.

The water crisis has fundamentally changed the lives of people in Flint, but it also had a rippling life-changing effect on those in Flint's orbit. As I have said, I consider myself an outsider to Flint. I didn't grow up there. I never lived there. I don't look like a lot of the people there. But I did spend significant time in Flint; my children spent much of their early childhood there, and the city holds a special place in my heart. I can say that my experience, while different from others' experiences, was no less life changing. The water crisis spurred me to learn more about Flint, to deepen my knowledge of place-based education in my field of social studies, and inspired a lot of reflection and learning about myself. That learning might not have been possible if not for my experience living through the water crisis. I believe that others can learn from Flint as I did.

WHAT I LEARNED ABOUT FLINT

The people of Flint have always been trailblazers for justice. Flint was the site of one of the most influential strikes of the labor movement in U.S. history (Loomis, 2018). In the 1970s, people in Flint fought for school integration, open housing, and clean air in their neighborhoods (Highsmith, 2015). Before the world knew about the water crisis, mothers in Flint were showing up to city council meetings with their children's bottles filled with brown water (Bebow, 2016). The country has been learning lessons from Flint for decades thanks to the sacrifices of those who live(d) there.

Flint was also once a leader in public education because of Frank Manley's community schools model. Educators the world over once looked to Flint as a model for community and school partnerships. This do-it-ourselves mentality has inspired educational leaders in Flint today. People like Jodi Ramos and Jacquie Richardson are Flint natives carrying on a tradition of community and school connections in their classrooms and schools. Despite individual educators working to improve public education for Flint's children, they're having a hard time moving the needle. It remains to be seen whether the new board of education members elected in 2022 will contribute to a more functioning group, or whether superintendent Kevelin Jones will be given support to lead the district. It may take more collective action among the community, such as when neighborhoods and parents came together to fight for clean water, to make a dent in the work. When schools are intertwined with the community, others may start to see that success for one is success for all. Place-based education can facilitate that.

Regardless of what the city of Flint demands for their children's education, it will be expensive. Special education services; community programming; hiring good teachers and incentivizing them to stay in the profession, and in Flint; facilitating partnerships with institutions in the city—all of this requires significant investments in education. If we learned any lessons from the state of Michigan's response to the water crisis, we learned that we can't always trust government officials to invest in what's best for communities. However, Flint is unique in that the legacy of C. S. Mott's wealth and commitment to education remains strong in the city. The Mott Foundation is ready to write checks to FCS or spend money on other educational entities like Educare and Flint Cultural Center Academy. The catch is that C. S. Mott's wealthy influence on education in Flint is complicated. His and Frank Manley's community schools model may have been incredibly influential and beneficial in some respects, but it also worked to uphold segregation and white supremacy in the community. At one time, the Mott Foundation essentially ran FCS, which raises questions about how "public" a school system is when bankrolled by a private foundation. When the Mott Foundation decided to stop funding community schools in the 1970s, it left FCS high and dry.

This complicated history between FCS and the Mott Foundation continues to be a present-day concern as the two groups still clash with each other. An outsider may look at this and be amazed that FCS wouldn't want to take the Mott Foundation's offers for money to improve education, but studying place on a deeper level shows the rationale behind it, as frustrating as it may seem. Although I have my share of skepticism about corporate interests and billionaires inserting themselves in public education under the "philanthropy" label, studying education in Flint has raised more questions for me and opened my mind. I believe that Educare and Flint Cultural Center Academy are doing good things for the community. I want Flint students to have filtered water in their school buildings that they can trust, as well as access to healthy food for free. In Flint, these things exist (or did exist) because of the Mott Foundation, as well as billionaires like Elon Musk and Tom Gores. It might be possible to create something place-based and attentive to community that is funded through philanthropy, but I also know that it might not be as easy as it sounds.

Solutions are never simple, but that isn't a reason to stop working to find them. Rachel Maddow, when covering the Flint water crisis for her MSNBC show, once asked if Flint was still habitable. I know that Maddow's dramatic reporting style is part of her charm to some, but I found this question offensive. There are, were, and always will be people in Flint, so what if we answered "no" to that question? What comes after that? Does our responsibility to make all parts of our country "habitable" end? The state government essentially assumed that Flint was inhabitable already when it allowed the water supply to become tainted with lead. But of course, Flint is habitable because people live there. And places are about people. And if I learned anything about Flint, I learned that there will always be "Flintstones" who carry stories of hopefulness and joy and who fight for justice through generations.

WHAT I LEARNED FROM FLINT ABOUT PLACE-BASED EDUCATION IN SOCIAL STUDIES

Place-based education helps both teachers and students better understand their communities. In social studies, this is particularly important because the attachment and awareness that comes from studying place allows us to take meaningful action in our communities and work for justice in a way that honors what the community needs. Listening and learning from the community also opens up learning from counternarratives to further develop critical thinking and empathy. Working in Flint helped me connect my knowledge of social studies inquiry with new understandings of place and place-based education.

The environmental racism of the water crisis is both highly specific to Flint and yet increasingly common, as our country's reliance on lead pipes decades ago and lack of investment in infrastructure up until recently has caused "a thousand Flints" (Highsmith, 2015, p. 23) all over the country (Lawson, 2023). Hearing about Jackson, Mississippi in 2022 brought up all kinds of memories of those early days of the water crisis in Flint (Adams, 2023). Being in Flint during this time taught me the importance of listening when it comes to "taking informed action." Flint residents were happy to have water bottle donations, surely, but they also demanded (and ultimately won) reparations for those who were harmed. Many residents were happy to have people finally become aware of the water crisis in 2016 but were also frustrated that it took so long, and they also refused to be seen as victims (Pauli, 2019). Residents fought for filters, but many still don't trust that they will work. A crisis is complicated—any "action" one might think a community needs may not be the right one. As more water crises happen in other places, it's important to listen and understand to know how to respond.

My time in Flint taught me how to develop my understanding. Listening is great, but it's only the first step. I can listen to South Parks residents speak of how disappointed they are that their neighborhood school closed, but if I don't understand the systemic spatial injustices that caused FCS to close more schools in Black neighborhoods than others, then I haven't fully understood the residents' feelings behind the closings. Understanding takes time. I also learned that the process of slowing down, immersing oneself in a place, and being present is really important to understanding communities.

In a literal sense, I saw place-based social studies happening in classrooms all over the city. I saw examples of educators and teacher educators treating the community as an extension of the classroom, and I saw firsthand how perspectives on the city changed as a result. I saw how my college students loved field trips through the city, and listened to Jacquie's stories about her middle schoolers taking care of the grounds around the Stockton House. I saw toddlers learning geography concepts on our campus and saw collaborative mapmaking of Flint's "special places" in Jen's preschool classroom. FCCA is in the middle of transforming into a place-based school around the Cultural Center, and early childhood administrators like Jodi are helping families through action informed by place and community need.

The subtitle of this book "Learning from Flint, Michigan" is both literal and figurative. There are many literal lessons we can take from Flint's experience with the water crisis, how the water crisis has impacted education in the city, and how people are responding to the community's needs. However, one of the more important figurative lessons we can learn from Flint is how to apply the study of place anywhere. At the end of each chapter, I have listed ways one can learn about place no matter where one ends up teaching. By talking about and pointing out the uniqueness of Flint, my hope is that this book inspires educators to think about social studies from the lens of what makes their place "their place."

WHAT I LEARNED FROM FLINT ABOUT MYSELF

As much as I learned about Flint and place-based education over the years, I learned just as much about myself as a social studies educator and a scholar during my time in Flint. As I am writing this, it's been 10 years since I finished a dissertation and more than a decade since I began teaching undergraduate social studies methods. The teacher and scholar I am now is almost unrecognizable from when I first stepped foot on the brick streets of Flint. This is all because of the people I interacted with over the years. My biggest realization is that place-based education is truly a transformative human experience. The people in Flint (residents, educators, my colleagues) either directly introduced me to new ways of knowing and thinking or inspired one of my rabbit holes of knowledge that developed me into a deeper social studies scholar and thinker. I learned more about place and place-based education from my secondary education colleagues at UM-Flint, more about early childhood social studies from daughters' teachers, and more about community activism from every Flint resident fighting for a better future for Flint's children.

And as I mentioned in the section above, I now feel equipped to apply this study of place anywhere. My Flint story has an ending now. I no longer work at UM-Flint. I moved back to my hometown in West Michigan and now work at another university in a completely new and different place. But my time in Flint equipped me with the tools I need to learn about this new place and gave me the knowledge and perspective I needed to see even the more familiar places over here in a new light.

CONCLUSION

"[P]lace is not so much a quality of things in the world but an aspect of the way we choose to think about it—what we decide to emphasize, and what we decide to designate as unimportant. This book is as much about place as a way of knowing as it is about place as a thing in the world" (Creswell, 2004, p.19).

Part of my journey in Flint was to see the city as more than just what Creswell (2004) describes as a "quality of things." If he is right, and *place* is how one chooses to think about it, I wanted to think about Flint in a different way than I had before. It's easy for some to emphasize the negativities about Flint. The state government clearly dismissed the city, as well its people, as unimportant. I chose to emphasize the city's assets, to critique the systemic issues that caused (and are still causing) the negativity, and to advocate for others. These are lessons I learned from the people in Flint.

More broadly, I want all educators to see place as beyond just a location where one's school happens to be. That school, that location, and that place have meanings that are impossible to separate. This will make us better social studies educators, better parents, and better citizens. Flint did that for me. Flint changed how I teach and how I parent. Flint changed my way of knowing. Flint changed my life.

References

Acosta, R. (2018, April 15). *Weather ball update bringing change to Flint skyline.* MLive. www.mlive.com/news/flint/2018/04/flint_skyline_changing_with_up.html

Adams, C. (2023, Jan 17). *Jackson, Mississippi's water crisis persists as national attention and help fade away.* NBC News. www.nbcnews.com/news/nbcblk/jackson-mississippi-still-dealing-water-crisis-rcna65563

Adams, D. (2013, May 12). *Half of closed Flint schools over last 10 years in predominantly black neighborhoods in northwest quadrant.* MLive. www.mlive.com/news/flint/2013/05/neighborhoods_around_closed_fl.html

Adams, D. (2015, October 8). *Toxic water in Flint schools is "mind-baffling," says elementary school parent.* MLive. www.mlive.com/news/flint/2015/10/parents_react_to_toxic_water_i.html

Ahmad, Z. (2019, Mar 26). *Planned grocery store would address "food desert" in Flint.* MLive. www.mlive.com/news/flint/2019/03/planned-grocery-store-would-address-food-desert-in-flint.html

American Montessori Society. (n.d.). *AMS Learning.* https://learn.amshq.org/abar-certificate-program

Arseven, A. (2014). The Reggio Emilia approach and curriculum development process. *International Journal of Academic Research, 6*(1), 166–171.

Artman-Meeker, K., & Kinder, K. A. (2016). The shoe project: Meaningful learning in an inclusive preschool classroom. *Social Studies and the Young Learner, 28*(4), 17–20.

Azizian, C. (2008, July 11). Community supporters made Flint Cultural Center a reality. *Flint Journal.* www.mlive.com/flintjournal/business/2008/07/community_supporters_made_flin.html

Banks, K. H., & Maixner, R. A. (2016). Social justice education in an urban charter Montessori school. *Journal of Montessori Research, 2*(2), 1–14.

Bebow, J. (2016). Timeline: 2004–2013. In B. Campbell (Ed.), *Poison on tap: How government failed Flint and the heroes who fought back* (pp. 26–32). Mission Point Press.

Blaisdell, B. (2017). Resisting redlining in the classroom: A collaborative approach to racial spaces analysis. In D. Morrison, S. A. Annamma, & D. D. Jackson (Eds.), *Critical race spatial analysis: Mapping to understand and address educational inequity* (pp. 109–125). Stylus Publishing.

Blankenship, W. G. (2018). Place. In D. G. Krutka, A. M. Whitlock, & M. Helmsing (Eds.), *Keywords in the social studies: Concepts and conversations* (pp. 99–100). Peter Lang Publishing.

Bondy, D. (2019, Aug 30). *Michigan near the top in the country for number of homeschoolers*. Mid-Michigan Now. https://midmichigannow.com/news/local/michigan-near-the-tops-in-number-of-home-schoolers#:~:text=The%20website%20A2Z%20Homeschooling.com,in%20the%20State%20of%20Michigan

Boy, G. A. (2013). *Orchestrating human-centered design*. Springer.

Brillante, P., & Mankiw, S. (2015). A sense of place: Human geography in the early childhood classroom. *Young Children, 70*(3), 2–9.

Britt, E. (2018). Oral history and the discursive construction of identity in Flint, Michigan. *Journal of Linguistic Anthropology, 28*(3), 252–272.

Broaddus, A. (2022, January 25). *Schools in Flint, Michigan, are sticking with remote learning indefinitely. Families say they're struggling to keep up*. CNN. www.cnn.com/2022/01/25/us/michigan-flint-schools-remote-learning-covid-19/index.html

Brophy, J., & Alleman, J. (2006). *Children's thinking about cultural universals*. Lawrence Erlbaum Associates.

Burke, M. N. (2016, March 15). EPA email: Let's not "go out on a limb" for Flint. *The Detroit News*. www.detroitnews.com/story/news/michigan/flint-water-crisis/2016/03/15/hearing-epa/81805068

Burroughs, S. (2002). Testy times for social studies. *Social Education, 66*(5), 315–318.

Butler, A., & Sinclair, K. A. (2020). Place matters: A critical review of place inquiry and space methods in education research. *Review of Research in Education, 44*(1), 64–96.

Byker, E. J., Good, A. J., & Williams, N. N. (2018). Community. In D. G. Krutka, A. M. Whitlock, & M. Helmsing (Eds.), *Keywords in the social studies: Concepts and conversations* (pp. 159–167). Peter Lang Publishing.

Campbell, C. M. (1972). Contributions of the Mott Foundation to the community education movement. *The Phi Delta Kappan, 54*(3), 195–197.

Carmody, S. (2017). *New preschool aimed at helping Flint kids exposed to lead*. Michigan Radio. www.michiganradio.org/education/2017-12-11/new-preschool-aimed-at-helping-flint-kids-exposed-to-lead

Carp, J. (2008). "Ground-truthing" representations of social space: Using Lefebvre's conceptual triad. *Journal of Planning Education and Research, 28*, 129–142.

Casey, E. M., DiCarlo, C. F., & Sheldon, K. L. (2019). Growing democratic citizenship competencies: Fostering social studies understandings through inquiry learning in the preschool garden. *Journal of Social Studies Research, 43*(4), 361–373.

Charles Stewart Mott Foundation. (2023). *What we do*. www.mott.org/work/

Choi, J. B. (2002). Globalization and culture. *Journal of Communication Inquiry, 26*(4), 446–450.

Christensen, L., Faith, C., & Stubblefield, E. (2006). Relearning social studies and democracy: Three teachers deconstructing a modified Reggio Emilia approach. *Journal of Social Studies Research, 30*(2), 10–17.

Clark, A. (2018). *The poisoned city*. Metropolitan Books.

Cochran-Smith, M. (1991). Learning to teach against the grain. *Harvard Education Review, 61*(3), 279–311.

Cooley, M. (2000). Human-centered design. In R. Jackson (Ed.), *Information design* (pp. 59–69). MIT Press.

Crenshaw, K. (1991). Mapping the margins: Intersectionality, identity politics, and violence against women of color. *Stanford Law Review, 43*(6), 1241–1299.
Creswell, T. (2004). *Place: A short introduction*. Blackwell Publishing.
Dani, D. (2019). A community and place-based approach to middle childhood science teacher education. *Middle School Journal, 50*(2), 45–52.
Darling-Hammond, L., & Oakes, J. (2019). *Preparing teachers for deeper learning*. Harvard Education Press.
Debs, M. (2015, March 12–15). *Racial and economic diversity in US public Montessori schools* [Poster presentation]. American Montessori Society Annual Conference, Philadelphia, PA.
Debs, M. (2019). *Diverse families, desirable schools: Public Montessori in the era of school choice*. Harvard Education Press.
Debs, M. C., & Brown, K. E. (2017). Students of color and public Montessori schools: A review of the literature. *Journal of Montessori Research, 3*(1), 1–15.
Decker, L. E. (1992). Building learning communities: Realities of educational restructuring. In L. E. Decker & V. A. Romney (Eds.), *Educational restructuring and the community education process* (pp. 5–12). Mid Atlantic Center for Community Education, Curry School of Education, University of Virginia.
Decker, L. E. (1999). *The evolution of the community school concept: The leadership of Frank J. Manley*. National Community Education.
Decker, L. E., & Romney, V. A. (Eds.). (1992). *Educational restructuring and the community education process*. National Coalition for Community Education.
Demarest, A. B. (2015). *Place-based curriculum design: Exceeding standards through local investigations*. Routledge.
Dewey, J. (1902/1990) *The school and society & the child and the curriculum*. The University of Chicago.
Dilberti, M. K., Woo, A., & Kaufman, J. H. (2023). *The missing infrastructure for elementary (K–5) social studies instruction: Findings from the 2022 American Instructional Resources Survey*. RAND Corporation. www.rand.org/pubs/research_reports/RRA134-17.html
Dorfman, A. B., & Kenney, C. K. (2020). Flint, Michigan through children's eyes: Using a teaching circle and projects to re-envision a city. *Early Childhood Education Journal, 48*(5), 573–584.
Dow, D. M. (2016). The deadly challenges of raising African American boys: Navigating the controlling image of the "thug." *Gender & Society, 30*(2), 161–188.
Dwyer, D. (2014, June 9). *The day Michigan killed public schools (and then created the system we have today)*. Michigan Radio. https://stateofopportunity.michiganradio.org/education/2014-06-09/the-day-michigan-killed-public-schools-and-then-created-the-system-we-have-today
Educare. (n.d). *The Educare model*. www.educareschools.org/our-approach/educare-model
Edwards, C., Gandini, L., & Forman, G. (Eds.). (2012). *The hundred languages of children: The Reggio Emilia experience in transformation* (3rd ed.). Praeger.
Erikson, D. (2022, December 5). *Aaron Bird Bear, set to retire, changed the way we understand campus*. WNews. https://news.wisc.edu/aaron-bird-bear-set-to-retire-changed-the-way-we-understand-campus
Fettes, M., & Judson, G. (2011). Imagination and the cognitive tools of place-making. *The Journal of Environmental Education, 42*(2), 123–135.

Flint Board of Education. (1958). Flint kindergartners look to a bright future. *Flint School Review, 10*(1), 1.

Flint Cultural Center. (2022). *Home.* flintcultural.org

Flint Public Schools can be the best. (1951, Feb). *Working together* (2nd ed.).

Fonger, R. (2015, October 16). *Detroit water begins flowing into Flint once again.* MLive. www.mlive.com/news/flint/2015/10/detroit_water_begins_flowing_i.html

Ford, H. C. (2022, Aug 22). Education beat: Tumult continues on Flint ed board as president, treasurer tossed. *East Village Magazine.* www.eastvillagemagazine.org/2022/08/22/education-beat-tumult-continues-on-flint-ed-board-as-president-treasurer-tossed

Genesee Intermediate School District. (2023). *Welcome to GISD.* www.geneseeisd.org

Gersmehl, P. (2014). *Teaching geography* (3rd ed.). The Guilford Press.

Glasson, R. R. (1951, December 12). Public likes first new school to be dedicated here in 22 years. *The Flint Journal.*

Goetz, D. (2021, July 22). *Mott Foundation reverses decision, will fund Flint school programs in 2021–22.* MLive. www.mlive.com/news/flint/2021/07/mott-foundation-reverses-decision-will-fund-flint-school-programs-in-2021-22.html

Goetz, D. (2022a, February 8). *Flint schools unveil Elon Musk–funded water fountains.* MLive. www.mlive.com/news/flint/2022/02/flint-schools-unveil-elon-musk-funded-water-fountains.html

Goetz, D. (2022b, April 5). *Flint school board member facing assault, disorderly charges after allegedly assaulting colleague.* MLive. www.mlive.com/news/flint/2022/04/flint-school-board-member-facing-assault-disorderly-charges-after-allegedly-assaulting-colleague.html

Goetz, D. (2022c, May 12). *Education community speaks out against possible closure of two Flint schools.* MLive. www.mlive.com/news/flint/2022/05/education-community-speaks-out-against-possible-closure-of-two-flint-schools.html

Goetz, D. (2022d, August 22). *Green agrees to resign from Flint school board after alleged assault of colleague.* MLive. www.mlive.com/news/flint/2022/08/green-agrees-to-resign-from-flint-school-board-after-alleged-assault-of-colleague.html

Goetz, D. (2022e, Nov 6). *In the past decade, Flint schools have lost 66% of their students.* MLive. www.mlive.com/news/flint/2022/11/in-past-decade-flint-schools-have-lost-66-of-their-students.html

Greater Flint Health Coalition (GFHC) & Pediatric Public Health Initiative (PPHI). (2023). *State of Flint kids: A resource for local data.* www.stateofflintkids.com/indicators

Gruenewald, D. (2003a). Foundations of place: A multidisciplinary framework for place-conscious education. *American Educational Research Journal, 40*(3), 619–654.

Gruenewald, D. (2003b). The best of both worlds: A critical pedagogy of place. *Education Researcher, 32*(4), 3–12.

Gustafson, A. (2023, March 21). *Judge gives final stamp of approval on $626m settlement for Flint water crisis victims.* Michigan Advance. https://michiganadvance.com/2023/03/21/judge-gives-final-stamp-of-approval-on-626m-settlement-for-flint-water-crisis-victims/#:~:text=Nearly%20a%20decade%20after%20the,million%20has%20been%20formally%20approved

Hanna-Attisha, M. (2018). *What the eyes don't see: A story of crisis, resistance, and hope in an American city*. One World.

Hayes, P. (2020, October 28). *I-475 is a relic of systemic racism, and if there's a way to get rid of it, Flint should*. Flintside. www.flintside.com/inthenews/flint-i-475-plan.aspx

Heafner, T. L., Lipscomb, G. B., & Rock, T. C. (2006). To test or not to test? The role of testing in elementary social studies. *Social Studies Research and Practice, 1*(2), 145–164.

Heckman, J. J. (2012). *Invest in early childhood development: Reduce deficits, strengthen the economy*. The Heckman Equation. http://heckmanequation.org

Heckman, J. J., & Karapakula, G. (2019). The Perry Preschoolers at late midlife: A study in design-specific interference [White paper]. Human Capital and Economic Opportunity Global Working Group.

Highsmith, A. R. (2012). Prelude to the subprime crash: Beecher, Michigan, and the origins of the suburban crisis. *The Journal of Policy History, 24*(4), 572–611.

Highsmith, A. R. (2015). *Demolition means progress: Flint, Michigan and the fate of the American metropolis*. University of Chicago Press.

Hinds, J. (2016, Feb 23). Top directors, performers to be in Flint on Oscar night. *Detroit Free Press*. www.freep.com/story/news/local/michigan/flint-water-crisis/2016/02/23/flint-oscar-night-fund-raiser/80802658

House, K. (2021, January 14). *Flint residents unimpressed by Snyder charges linked to lead poisoning*. Bridge Magazine. www.bridgemi.com/michigan-environment-watch/flint-residents-unimpressed-snyder-charges-linked-lead-poisoning

Jackson, Z. (2018, July 23). *Flint Cultural Center details how arts millage money would be spent*. MLive. www.mlive.com/news/flint/2018/07/flint_cultural_center_addresse.html

Jones, S. (2023). *Montessori vs. Reggio Emilia: Similarities and differences*. Montessori for Today. https://montessorifortoday.com/montessori-vs-reggio-emilia-similarities-and-differences

Jor'dan, J. R. (2018). Predominantly Black institutions and public Montessori schools: Reclaiming the "genius" in African American children. *Multicultural Learning and Teaching, 13*(1), 1–7.

Jordan, D. (2021, October 21). U-M's 2021 fall enrollment tops 50,000 for first time. *The University Record*. https://record.umich.edu/articles/u-m-enrollment-this-fall-tops-50000-for-first-time

Keefer, W. (2019, July 16). *Flint schools gear up for August start to balanced calendar year*. MLive. www.mlive.com/news/flint/2019/07/flint-schools-gear-up-for-august-start-to-balanced-calendar-year.html

Keefer, W. (2022, January 18). *Flint continues to grapple with rising homicide rate, violent crimes in 2021*. MLive. www.mlive.com/news/flint/2021/12/flint-continues-to-grapple-with-rising-homicide-violent-crime-rates-in-2021.html

Keith, N. Z. (1996). Can urban school reform and community development be joined? The potential of community schools. *Education and Urban Society, 28*(2), 237–268.

Kilpatrick, W. H. (1914). *The Montessori system examined*. Houghton Mifflin.

Kilpatrick, W. H. (1918). The project method. *Teacher's College Record, 19*, 319–334.

Kitchens, J. (2009). Situated pedagogy and the Situationist International: Countering a pedagogy of placelessness. *Educational Studies, 45*, 240–261.

Knight, S., McLeman, L., Salvador, K., De La Mare, D. M., & Hiramatsu, K. (2018). Building the house while we're living in it: Conceptualizing place-based teacher education. *National Teacher Education Journal, 11*(2), 5–14.

Korte, G. (2016, May 4). Obama drinks Flint water as he urges children to be tested for lead. *USA Today.* www.usatoday.com/story/news/politics/2016/05/04/obama-flint-visit-drinking-water-lead-poisoning/83916778

Krajewski, F., & Osowski, V. (1997). The National Center for Community Education: On the threshold of a new age. *Mott Exchange, 12*(2).

Ladson-Billings, G. (1995). Toward a theory of culturally relevant pedagogy. *American Educational Research Journal, 32*(3), 465–491.

Ladson-Billings, G. (2021). I'm here for the hard re-set: Post pandemic pedagogy to preserve our culture. *Equity & Excellence in Education, 54*(1), 68–78.

Landry, L. (2020, Dec 15). What is human-centered design? *Harvard Business Review.* https://online.hbs.edu/blog/post/what-is-human-centered-design

Latz, A. O. (2017). *Photovoice research in education and beyond: A practical guide from theory to exhibition*. Routledge.

Lave, J., & Wenger, E. (1991). *Situated learning: Legitimate peripheral participation*. Cambridge University Press.

Lawson, J. (2023, April 19). *Lead in the water: How some of America's water became too dangerous to drink*. ABC News. https://abcnews.go.com/US/lead-water-americas-water-dangerous-drink/story?id=98438736

Levin, K. (2022, April 12). *Returning homeschoolers, kindergarteners drive Michigan enrollment rebound*. Chalkbeat Detroit. https://detroit.chalkbeat.org/2022/4/12/23022749/michigan-pandemic-enrollment-rebound-trends-homeschool

Loewen, J. W. (2007). *Lies my teacher told me: Everything your American history textbook got wrong*. Simon & Schuster.

Loomis, E. (2018). *A history of America in ten strikes*. The New Press.

Lowenstein, E., Grewal, I. K., Erkaeva, N., Nielsen, R., & Voelker, L. (2018). Place-based teacher education: A model whose time has come. *Issues in Teacher Education, 27*(2), 36–52.

Maguth, B. M., & Hilburn, J. (2011). The community as a learning laboratory: Using place-based education to foster a global perspective in the social studies. *The Ohio Social Studies Review, 47*(1), 27–34.

Malaguzzi, L. (1996). *The hundred languages of children: The Reggio Emilia approach to early childhood education*. Ablex Publishing Corporation.

Martell, C. C., & Stevens, K. M. (2019). Culturally sustaining social studies teachers: Understanding models of practice. *Teaching and Teacher Education, 86*, 1–11.

Mazama, A. (2016). African American homeschooling practices: Empirical evidence. *Theory and Research in Education, 14*(1) 26–44.

Michigan Department of Education. (2019). *Michigan K–12 standards social studies*. Michigan Department of Education.

MI Lead Safe. (2023). *Learn about lead*. State of Michigan. www.michigan.gov/mileadsafe

Michigan Senate Fiscal Agency (MISFA). (n.d.). *FY 2018–19 Resident undergraduate tuition and fee rates*. www.senate.michigan.gov/sfa/Departments/DataCharts/DChed_TuitionFees.pdf

Mitchell, C. (2019, August 26). *In Flint, schools overwhelmed by special ed. needs in aftermath of lead crisis*. Education Week. www.edweek.org/teaching-learning/in-flint-schools-overwhelmed-by-special-ed-needs-in-aftermath-of-lead-crisis/2019/08

Moll, L. C., Amanti, C., Neff, D., & González, N. (1992). Funds of knowledge for teaching: Using a qualitative approach to connect homes and classrooms. *Theory Into Practice, 31*(2), 132–141.

Montessori, M. (1912). *The Montessori method: Scientific pedagogy as applied to child education in the "Children's Houses" with additions and revisions by the author*. Frederick A. Stokes Company.

Morrison, D., Annamma, S. A., & Jackson, D. D. (Eds.). (2017). *Critical race spatial analysis: Mapping to understand and address educational inequality*. Stylus.

Mott program upped to $400,000. (1953, August 20). *The Flint Journal*.

Mulvihill, K. (2021). *Causes and effects of lead in water*. National Resources Defense Council. www.nrdc.org/stories/causes-and-effects-lead-water#:~:text=High%20lead%20levels%20have%20been,isn't%20limited%20to%20cities

Murray, A. K., Davis, D. M., & Ellerbeck, S. A. (2021). Montessori education in Kansas City, Missouri, from 1988–2005: Race, the Dottoressa, and the pink tower. *American Educational History Journal, 48*, 43–63.

Murray, A. K., Johnston, L. C., Sabater, A., & Clark, K. (2020). Hidden Black voices in the history of Montessori education. *American Educational History Journal, 47*(1–2), 205–215.

National Center for Education Statistics (NCES). (n.d.). *Race and ethnicity of public school teachers and their students*. https://nces.ed.gov/pubs2020/2020103/index.asp

National Council for the Social Studies (NCSS). (2008). A vision of powerful teaching and learning in the social studies: Building effective citizens. *Social Education, 72*(5), 277–280.

National Council for the Social Studies (NCSS). (2013). *College, career, and civic life (C3) framework for social studies*. National Council for the Social Studies.

National Resource Defense Council (NRDC). (2020, Mar 29). Michigan to reconnect homes to water, end shut-offs during COVID-19 crisis [Press release]. www.nrdc.org/media/2020/200329

Nesbitt, C. (2020, December 10). *Flint kids with disabilities receive $9 million as part of water crisis settlement*. FlintBeat. https://flintbeat.com/flint-kids-with-disabilities-receive-9-million-as-part-of-water-crisis-settlement

Nesbitt, C. (2022, April 4). *Flint Public Art Project showcases student poetry inspired by Flint murals*. Flintbeat. https://flintbeat.com/flint-public-art-project-showcases-students-poems-inspired-by-flint-murals

Noddings, N. (2002). *Starting at home: Caring and social policy*. University of California Press.

Noel, J. (2016). Community-based urban teacher education: Theoretical frameworks and practical considerations for developing promising practices. *The Teacher Educator, 51*(4), 335–350.

Nxumalo, F. (2019). *Decolonizing place in early childhood education*. Routledge.

Oakes, J., Maier, A., & Daniel, J. (2017). *Community schools: An evidence-based strategy for equitable school improvement*. National Education Policy Center.

Orr, D. (1994). *Earth in mind*. Island Press.

Oshio, T., & Kupperman, J. (2021). The problem behind the problem: Applying human-centered design to childcare in Flint. *Early Childhood Education Journal, 50*, 1373–1382.

Paris, D., & Alim, H. S. (2014). What are we seeking to sustain through culturally sustaining pedagogy? A loving critique forward. *Harvard Educational Review, 84*(1), 85–100.

Pauli, B. J. (2019). *Flint fights back: Environmental justice and democracy in the Flint Water Crisis*. The MIT Press.

Payne, K. A. (2015). Who can fix this? The concept of "audience" and first graders' civic agency. *Social Studies and the Young Learner, 27*(4), 19–22.

Pierret, A. (2021, August 23). *Flint Community Schools closed all week due to excessive heat in buildings*. ABC12News. www.abc12.com/news/education/flint-community-schools-closed-all-week-due-to-excessive-heat-in-buildings/article_f09c35ee-5db4-570c-91d8-63573b552bd9.html

Popielarz, K., & Galliher, A. (2023). Developing accountability and responsibility: How teacher candidates experience and conceptualize community-based pedagogy in the social studies. *Theory and Research in Social Education, 51*(1), 100–127.

Private School Review. (2023). *Grand Blanc Montessori*. www.privateschoolreview.com/grand-blanc-montessori-profile

Provider Empowerment Program. (2020). *Food, clothing, health care and other assistance*. https://pep-flint.org/food-clothing-and-other-assistance

Public School Montessorian. (2005). Parent pressure keeps two programs intact. *Public School Montessorian, 17*(4), 14.

Public School Review. (2023a). *Burton Glen Charter Academy quick stats*. www.publicschoolreview.com/michigan/burton-glen-charter-academy-school-district/2600251-school-district

Public School Review. (2023b). *Linden Charter Academy quick stats*. www.publicschoolreview.com/linden-charter-academy-profile

Ray, B. (2015). African American homeschool parents' motivations for homeschooling and their Black children's academic achievement. *Journal of School Choice, 9*(1), 71–96.

Reggio Emilia Approach. (2022). *Values*. www.reggiochildren.it/en/reggio-emilia-approach/valori-en

Resor, C. W. (2010). Place-based education: What is its place in the social studies classroom? *The Social Studies, 101*(5), 185–188.

Richardson, J. (2009). *The full-service community school movement: Lessons from the James Adams Community School*. Palgrave Macmillan.

Rodríguez, N. N., & Swalwell, K. (2021). *Social studies for a better world: An anti-oppressive approach for elementary educators*. W. W. Norton.

Rogovin, P. (2015). Kindergartners' questions become the curriculum. *Social Studies and the Young Learner, 28*(1), 8–11.

Rohrer, H., & Cady, D. (1992). Community education: Adapting to the needs of an urban community. In L. E. Decker & V. A. Romney (Eds.), *Educational restructuring and the community education process* (pp. 107–110). Mid Atlantic Center for Community Education, Curry School of Education, University of Virginia.

References

Roth, A. (2020, October 21). *Whitmer "sounding the alarm bell" as COVID-19 reaches new peak in Michigan*. Flintbeat. https://flintbeat.com/whitmer-sounding-the-alarm-bell-as-covid-19-reaches-new-peak-in-michigan

Ruth Mott Foundation. (2021). *Our founder & mission*. www.ruthmottfoundation.org/about-us/our-founder-and-mission/

Ryan, J. B., Katsiyannis, A., Counts, J. M., & Shelnut, J. C. (2018). The growing concerns regarding school resource officers. *Intervention in School and Clinic, 53*(3), 188–192.

Sanders, M. (2016). Leadership, partnerships, and organizational development: Exploring components of effectiveness in three full-service community schools. *School Effectiveness and School Improvement, 27*(2), 157–177.

Schirra, C. R. (2022, January 26). Lead in drinking water: Change (and opportunity!) on the horizon. *Insights and Resources*. www.bricker.com/insights-resources/publications/lead-in-drinking-water-change-and-opportunity-on-the-horizon

Schmidt, L. (2007). *Social studies that sticks: How to bring content and concepts to life*. Heinemann.

Seneschal, E. (2007). Environmental justice in Egleston Square. In D. Gruenewald & G. Smith (Eds.), *Place-based education in the global age* (pp. 85–11). Taylor & Francis.

Smith, G. A., & Sobel, D. (2010). *Place- and community-based education in schools*. Routledge.

Sobel, D. (1998). *Mapmaking with children: Sense-of-place education for the elementary years*. Heinemann.

Sobel, D. (2005). *Place-based education: Connecting classrooms and communities*. Orion Society.

Soja, E. W. (2010). *Seeking spatial justice*. University of Minnesota Press.

Stebbins, L. G. (2020, March 18). *Hanna-Attisha: Any lead testing results in Flint kids underestimate exposure*. Michigan Advance. https://michiganadvance.com/2020/03/18/hanna-attisha-any-lead-testing-results-in-flint-kids-underestimate-exposure

Stebbins, S. (2022). *Flint, MI reported one of the highest murder rates in the US*. 24/7 Wall St. https://247wallst.com/city/flint-mi-reported-one-of-the-highest-murder-rates-in-the-us

Stephenson, M. E. (1997). Dr. Maria Montessori—A contemporary educator? In The relevance of Montessori today: Meeting human needs—principles to practice [Conference proceedings]. American Montessori International of the United States, Bellevue, WA, July 25–28, 1996.

Tenneriello, T. (2022). *Competition in public education: A case study on a Michigan charter school's perspective* [Unpublished doctoral dissertation]. University of Michigan-Flint.

Thacker, E. S., & Bodle, A. T. (2022). Seizing the moment: A critical place-based partnership for antiracist elementary social studies teacher education. *Theory and Research in Social Education, 50*(3), 402–430.

Thorne, B. (2014, May 23). *See how Flint's population has changed over 150 years*. MLive. www.mlive.com/news/flint/2014/05/see_how_flints_population_has.html

Todd, R. H., & Brinkman, S. G. (2007). Service learning in a social studies methods course: Experience and place-based curriculum. *The Educational Forum, 72*(1), 79–91.

Trierweiler, G. (2014). An overview of Family Star Montessori School. *The NAMTA Journal, 39*(2), 123–130.

Trujillo, T. M., Hernández, L. E., Jarrell, T., & Kissell, R. (2014). Community schools as urban district reform: Analyzing Oakland's policy landscape through oral histories. *Urban Education, 49*(8), 895–929.

Tuck, E., & McKenzie, M. (2015). *Place in research: Theory, methodology, and methods.* Routledge.

United States Census Bureau. (n.d.a). *Place: Beecher CDP, Michigan.* https://data.census.gov/profile/Beecher_CDP,_Michigan?g=1600000US2606820

United States Census Bureau. (n.d.b). *Quick facts: Flint city, Michigan.* www.census.gov/quickfacts/fact/table/US/PST045221

University of Michigan. (2021, November 1). *The problem behind the problem: Applying human-centered design to childcare in Flint* [Video]. YouTube. www.youtube.com/watch?v=ZVmwtoBzsPY&t=216s

University of Michigan-Flint. (2023). *Institutional analysis.* www.umflint.edu/ia/campus-statistics/university-overview

Urioste, M. (2014). Multicultural inclusion in an urban setting. *The NAMTA Journal, 39*(3), 65–88.

U.S. News and World Report. (2022). *Overview of the city of Flint school district.* www.usnews.com/education/k12/michigan/districts/flint-school-district-of-the-city-of-100623

U.S. News and World Report. (2023). *University of Michigan—Ann Arbor.* www.usnews.com/best-colleges/university-of-michigan-ann-arbor-9092#:~:text=Overview,campus%20size%20is%203%2C207%20acres

Vélez, V. N., & Solórzano, D. G. (2017). Critical race spatial analysis: Conceptualizing GIS as a tool for critical race research in education. In D. Morrison, S. A. Annamma, & D. D. Jackson (Eds.), *Critical race spatial analysis: Mapping to understand and address educational inequity* (pp. 8–31). Stylus Publishing.

Walker, B. (2021, June 2). *Homeschooling in Michigan jumped during pandemic.* The Center Square. www.thecentersquare.com/michigan/homeschooling-in-michigan-jumped-during-pandemic/article_90b02ad8-c3c9-11eb-af99-3fcad8fa7246.html#:~:text=According%20to%20U.S.%20Census%20data,6%20percentage%20points%20to%2011.3%25

Wang, J. (2019, May 14). *Preschool education can benefit generations of families.* UChicago News. https://news.uchicago.edu/story/preschool-education-can-benefit-generations-families

Watson, M., & Musa, A. (2022, December 13). *Criminal charges against former Michigan Gov. Rick Snyder related to Flint water crisis to be dismissed.* CNN News. www.cnn.com/2022/12/13/us/flint-michigan-rick-snyder-water-crisis/index.html#:~:text=Snyder%20was%20previously%20indicted%20in,the%20state's%20penal%20code%20shows

Whitlock, A. M. (2015). Economics through inquiry: Creating social businesses in fifth grade. *The Social Studies, 106*(3), 117–125.

Whitlock, A. M. (2017). Teaching about social business: The intersection of economics instruction and civic engagement. *Journal of Social Studies Research, 41*(3), 235–242.

Whitlock, A. M. (2020). Walking the city: Developing place-consciousness through inquiry. *Social Studies and the Young Learner, 33*(2), 20–24.

Whitlock, A. M., & Brugar, K. A. (2017). How does a cowboy make money? Using student questions to further elementary school inquiries. *The Social Studies, 108*(3), 79–86.

Whitlock, A. M., & Fox, K. (2014). One hen: Using children's literature in project-based learning. *Social Studies and the Young Learner, 26*(4), 26–29.

Yosso, T. J. (2005). Whose culture has capital? A critical race theory discussion of community cultural wealth. *Race and Ethnicity Education, 8*(1), 69–91.

Yosso, T. J., Smith, W. A., Ceja, M., & Solórzano, D. G. (2009). Critical race theory, racial microaggressions, and campus racial climate for Latina/o undergraduates. *Harvard Educational Review, 79*(4), 659–690.

Zeichner, K. (2010). Rethinking connections between campus courses and field experiences in college- and university-based teacher education. *Journal of Teacher Education, 61*(1–2), 89–99.

Zoltowski, C. B., Oakes, W. C., & Cardella, M. E. (2013). Students' ways of experiencing human-centered design. *Journal of Engineering Education, 101*(1), 28–59.

Zygmunt, E., & Clark, P. (2016). *Transforming teacher education for social justice.* Teacher's College Press.

Index

Accountability movement (21st century), 81
Acosta, R., 59
Adams, C., 142
Adams, D., 26, 27, 40
Ahmad, Z., 50
Alim, H. S., 105
Alleman, J., 130
Ambrose, Jerry, 6, 9
American Montessori Society, 78, 79, 82, 87
Anti-racist, anti-bias (ABAR) professional development, 82. *See also* Racism
Arseven, A., 68
Artman-Meeker, K., 72
Azizian, C., 93

Balanced school calendars, 38, 94
Banks, K. H., 79
Bebow, J., 5, 6, 140
Beecher, Michigan, 115–116
Bird Bear, Aaron, 131
Blaisdell, B., 49
Blankenship, W. G., 69
Bodle, A. T., 123
Bondy, D., 92
Boy, G. A., 55
Brillante, P., 62, 63, 72
Brinkman, S. G., 123
Broaddus, A., 38, 39
Brophy, J., 130
Brown, K. E., 80, 87
Brown, Mike, 4
Brugar, K. A., 71
Burke, M. N., 26
Burroughs, S., 81
Butler, A., 19, 31, 130, 136
Byker, E. J., 15, 17

Cady, D., 34, 35
Calendars, balanced, 38, 94
Campbell, C. M., 17
Carp, J., 43
Casey, Erin, 61, 73
Charles Stewart Mott Foundation. *See* Mott Foundation
Charter schools, 84, 89–99
Childcare, 47–48, 50, 52–54, 55–57
Choi, J. B., 15
Christensen, L., 73–74
Clark, A., 11
Clark, P., 105, 107, 123
Clinton, Bill, 7
Clinton, Hillary, 7
Cobleigh, Marissa, 51
Cochran-Smith, M., 106
Collaborative leadership, 41–42, 97–98
College, Career, and Civic Life Framework (NCSS), 104, 131
Community cultural wealth, 105
Community engagement, 39–40
Community School Director (CSD) position, 39
Community school movement, 16–20, 54
   extended learning time, 38–39
   in Flint, Michigan, 96–97
   Freeman Elementary, 27, 29
   in twenty-first century, 34–35
Cooley, M., 55
Copeny, Mari, 68–69
Co-teaching, 110–112
COVID-19 pandemic, 9–10, 33, 35, 38, 95
Cozart, Jen, 59–60, 68
Crenshaw, K., 15
Creswell, T., xvii, 11, 17, 144
Crim, Bobby, 34
Crim Foundation, 34–35, 39
Critical geography, 133–134
Critical place inquiry, xvii–xviii, 20–22, 30–32, 48
Critical race spatial analysis (CRSA), 19
Crow, Carl, 11
Culturally relevant pedagogy, 105

Dani, D., 106
Darling-Hammond, Linda, 117–118
Debs, M., 79, 80, 82, 86
Decker, L. E., 16, 17, 18, 19, 27, 34, 39, 48
De La Mare, Danielle, 110–111

Del Toral, Miguel, 7
Demarest, Amy B., 61, 97, 133
Demolition Means Progress (Highsmith), 3–4
Desegregation. *See also* Racism
　and Montessori schools, 81–82
　and Mott Foundation, 20, 25, 41
Dewey, John, 18, 20
Dilberti, M. K., 97
Discovering PLACE, 27–28
Dorfman, A. B., 71
Dow, D. M., 56
Dwyer, D., 91

Ealy, Darnell, 9
Early Childhood Development Center, UM-Flint (ECDC), 47–48, 52, 59–60, 63–65
　preschoolers' narratives, 67–71
　Teaching Strategies (TS) Gold assessment, 65–66
Early childhood education, 47–57
　Educare model, 52–53
　human-centered design, 54–57
　Reggio Emilia classrooms, 60–66
Early Head Start, 52
Eastern Michigan University (EMU), 106–107
Educare, 52–54, 57
Edwards, C., 60
Edwards, Marc, 7, 26
Engagement, family and community, 39–40
Engler, Governor John, 91
Environmental Protection Agency (EPA), 5, 7, 26, 49
Erikson, D., 131

Family engagement, 39–40
Fettes, M., 62
FFN (Family, Friend, and Neighbor) providers, 54–57
Field trips, 127–130
Flint, Michigan
　AutoWorld, 121–122
　background, overview, and statistics, 2, 10–11, 15, 48–49
　charter schools, 89–99
　community, sense of, 15
　Educare Flint, 53–54
　education in, history of, 16–22
　Flint as "third teacher" in Reggio Approach, 65–66
　food deserts and nutrition access, 50, 53
　Freeman Elementary School, 23–24, 26–29

Flint, Michigan (*continued*)
  Genesee Power Station, 3
  history and overview, 140–141
  Kindergarten choices, 94–95
  Montessori education, 83–88
  Pierce Elementary School, 36, 39–40, 93
  preschoolers' narratives, 67–71
  school segregation, 25–26
  segregation, 3–4, 24–25
  stereotypes and misconceptions, 124–125
  Stockton House Museum, 103–105
  YouthQuest, 41
Flint Center for Educational Excellence, 34
Flint Cultural Center, 92–93
Flint Cultural Center Academy (FCCA), 92, 93–99
Flint Farmers' Market, 28, 50, 60, 68, 127–128, 133, 134
Flint Fights Back (Pauli), 1
Flint Institute of Arts, 16
Flint Master Plan, 2, 6, 34
Flint Public Schools Can Be the Best, 17
Flint Southwestern High School, 112–114
Flint water crisis, 1–2, 5–7, 139–140
  community reactions, 8–10, 26
  response to, 125–127
  transition to river as water source, 3, 4–5
Fonger, Ron, 5, 26
Ford, H. C., 42
Fox, K., 104
Freeman, Ralph, 26
Funds of knowledge, 105

Gadpaille, Mae Arlene, 80
Galliher, A., 123
General Motors (GM), 20, 24, 93, 134
Genesee Intermediate School District (GISD), 27, 50, 51, 52, 53
Geography, 133–134
  critical place inquiry, 30–32
  themes of, xvii, 62
Gersmehl, P., xvii, 30, 62, 66, 122
Glasson, R. R., 26
Goetz, D., 36, 40, 41, 42, 92, 95
Gores, Tom, 50, 141
Gorman, Michael, 92
Grace, Shamarion, 36, 39–40, 42, 44, 93
Greater Flint Health Coalition (GFHC), 50, 51, 80
Great Lakes Stewardship Initiative (GLSI), 106–107, 123

Great Start Readiness Program (GSRP), 50, 52–53, 59–60
Green, Danielle, 42
Ground-truthing, 43–44, 55, 134
Gruenewald, D., 11, 62, 69, 79, 87, 97, 123, 127

Hanna-Attisha, Dr. Mona, 6, 7, 11, 23, 26, 28, 37, 49
Hayes, P., 25
Head Start, 52, 53, 54
Heafner, T. L., 81
Health care, school-based, 53
Heck, Linda, 112–114
Heckman, James, 50, 51, 79, 80
Henthorn, Tom, 128
Highsmith, Andrew, 3–4, 11, 19–20, 24, 25, 31, 41, 115, 121, 124, 140, 142
Hilburn, J., 122
Hinds, J., 7
Homeowner's Loan Corporation (HOLC) maps, 31
Homeschooling, 83, 92
House, K., 9
Human-centered design, 55–56, 57
Hypoxic ischemic encephalopathy (HIE), 47–48

Inquiry Arc, 21, 72
Inquiry-based learning, 10, 71–73
  early childhood, 48
Integrated student supports, 35–38, 51
Integration. *See* Desegregation

Jackson, Z., 93
Jamerson, Ja'Nel, 53
Jones, Kevelin, 38, 42, 140
Jones, S., 60
Jordan, D., 124
Jordan, Elizabeth, 83–86
Jor'dan, J. R., 80, 83, 87
Judson, G., 62
Justice-oriented education, 87–88, 106, 117. *See also* Spatial injustice

Karapakula, G., 50, 51, 79
Keefer, W., 38, 65
Keith, N. Z., 43
Kenney, Christine, 71, 73
Kilpatrick, William Heard, 18, 78–79
Kinder, K. A., 72
Kitchens, J., 123, 127
Knight, Suzanne, 108, 115, 116, 117, 120

Korte, G., 7
Krajewski, F., 16
Kupperman, Jeff, 54, 55
Kurtz, Ed, 4

Ladson-Billings, Gloria, 48, 60, 105
Landry, L., 55
Latz, A. O., 68, 74, 128
Laube, Heather, 83
Lave, J., 106
Lawson, J., 142
Lead Copper Rule (LCR), 49, 139
Lead poisoning, 49–50
  impact on early childhood education, 48–52
  impact on education, 37–38
  recovery from, 50–52
Learning Policy Institute, 35
  integrated student supports, 35–38
Levin, K., 92
Lieske, Eric, 93–94, 95–96, 97–99
Life skills, 78
Loewen, J. W., 19
Loomis, E., 134, 140
Lopez, Derrick, 42, 85
Lowenstein, E., 106, 107

Maddow, Rachel, 141
Maguth, B. M., 122
Maixner, R. A., 79
Malaguzzi, Loris, 60, 68, 74
Mankiw, S., 62, 63, 72
Manley, Frank, 16, 17, 18–19, 25, 34, 39, 96, 140–141
Mapmaking activities, 66, 70–71, 73
Mapmaking with Children (Sobel), 89
Martell, C. C., 105
Mattern, Carrie, 74–75
Mazama, A. A., 92
McDonnell, Sara, 111
McKenzie, M., xvii, 11, 48
McLeman, Laura, 112–116
Michigan
  accountability system, 81
  education standards, 20–21
  Michigan Charter School Act (1994), 91
  MI Lead Safe, 49
  schools-of-choice law, 91–92

Mitchell, C., 37
Moll, L. C., 105
Montessori, Dr. Maria, 77
Montessori education
  background, 77–78
  benefits of, 79–80
  in Flint, Michigan, 83–88
  place-based education, 78–79
  public funding of, 80
  public Montessori schools, 81–83
  and racial integration, 79–80
  and spatial injustices, 81–82
The Montessori Method (Montessori), 78
Morrison, D., 19
Mott, Charles Stewart (C. S.), 16, 19, 20, 25, 34, 41, 92–93, 141
Mott Foundation, 16–20, 25, 34–35, 41, 52, 93
Mulvihill, K., 31
Murray, A. K., 78, 80, 81, 82, 83
Musa, A., 9
Musk, Elon, 36, 141

National Council for the Social Studies (NCSS), 10, 21, 62, 72, 123
  College, Career and Civic Life Framework (C3), 104, 131
National Heritage Academies (NHA), 90
National Resource Defense Council (NRDC), 10
Nesbitt, C., 37, 75
Noddings, N., 135
Noel, J., 105, 106
Nxumalo, Fikile, 61, 62, 120

Oakes, Jeannie, 35, 36, 39, 41, 83, 117–118
Obama, Barack, 7
Oshio, Toko, 54, 55–56
Osowski, V., 16

Paris, D., 105
Pauli, Ben, 1, 4, 5, 11–12, 30, 142
Payne, K. A., 72
"Pedagogy of place," 10, 62, 123
Pierret, A., 38
Place, as theme of geography, xvii, 62
Place-based education, 10–12
  design, 57
  Discovering PLACE, 27–28
  Flint, Michigan charter school, 89–99
  Flint Cultural Center Academy (FCCA), 98–99

Place-based education (*continued*)
  and human-centered design, 55
  impact on author, 142–143
  implementation, 73–75
  Montessori Approach, 78–79
  Reggio Emilia education, 60–66
  and school improvement, 43–44
  and teacher preparation, UM-Flint, 107–110
Place-based social studies
  critical geography, 133–134
  field trips, 127–130
  in Flint, Michigan, 121–122
  methods, 122–127
  "Right Under Our Noses" Flint assignment, 121–122, 130–133, 136
  teacher preparation, 134–136
Place-based teacher education (PBTE), 105–107, 110, 116–118
Popielarz, K., 123
Preparing Teachers for Deeper Learning (Darling-Hammond & Oakes), 117
Preservice teachers. *See* Teacher education
Private School Review, 77
Progressive Era education, 18
Project-based learning, 10, 18, 78
Provider Empowerment Programs (PEPs), 55–56
Public School Review, 91

Racism, 19
  anti-racist, anti-bias (ABAR) professional development, 82
  housing segregation, 3–4, 24–25
  racial segregation, 19–20
  and school closures, 40
  school segregation, 25–26
Ramos, Jodi, 52, 53, 54, 140, 143
Ray, B., 92
Reggio Emilia Approach, 60–62
  inquiry-based learning, 71–73
  place-based classrooms, 62–66
  preschoolers' narratives, 67–71
Resor, C. W., 122
Rett-Henry, Starletta, 51, 81, 85, 87
Richardson, Jacquie, 23, 27–28, 36, 37, 42, 61, 103–105, 130, 140, 142–143
"Right Under Our Noses" Flint assignment, 121–122, 130–133, 136
Rodríguez, N. N., 131, 135
Rogovin, P., 72
Rohrer, H., 34, 35
Romney, V. A., 16, 18, 19
Roth, A., 10

Ruth Mott Foundation, 19
Ryan, J. B., 17

Salinas, Maria, 115–116
Sanders, Bernie, 7
Sanders, M., 35, 42
Schirra, C. R., 49
Schmidt, L., 18
Schools-of-choice law, Michigan, 91–92
Segregation. *See* Desegregation; Racism
Seneschal, E., 123
Sinclair, K. A., 19, 31, 130, 136
Smith, Gregory, 61, 89
Smith, Jacob, 103
Smith, Sincere, 30
Snyder, Governor Rick, 4, 9, 91, 116, 118
Sobel, David, 10, 61, 62, 66, 87, 89
Social-emotional learning, 39, 51–52
Soja, Edward, 26, 30, 134, 135
Solórzano, D. G., 43, 55, 134
Southeast Michigan Stewardship (SEMIS) Coalition, 106–107
Spatial injustice, 26, 56, 142. *See also* Justice-oriented education; Racism
    early childhood education, access to, 79
    examples, 31
    and Montessori education, 81–82
Stebbins, L. G., 37
Stebbins, S., 65
Stephenson, M. E., 77, 79, 87
Stevens, K. M., 105
Steward, Anita, 23, 42, 98
Stockton, Maria, 103–104
Stockton, Thomas, 103
Swalwell, Katy, 131, 135

Tawaab, Bilal, 36, 42, 84, 86
Teacher preparation
    field experiences, 112–114
    lesson planning, 130–131
    place-based, 105–107, 116–118, 134–136
    social foundations coursework, 114–116
    University of Michigan-Flint, 107–110, 118–120
Teaching Strategies (TS) Gold, 65
Tenneriello, T., 98
Thacker, E. S., 123
"Third teacher" in Reggio Approach, 61, 65–66
Thorne, B., 15

Todd, R. H., 123
Toddler classrooms, 62–66. *See also* Early childhood education
Trierweiler, G., 80, 82, 83
Trujillo, T. M., 35
Trump, Donald, 7
Tuck, E., xvii, 11, 48

United Auto Workers (UAW), 20, 134
University of Michigan-Flint, 124–125
   enrollment decline, 118
   teacher preparation, 107–110, 118–120
Urioste, M., 80, 82, 83

Vélez, V. N., 43, 55, 134
vocational education, 20

Walker, B., 92
Walks with students, 128–129
   preschoolers, 63–65
Walling, Dayne, 5
Walters, Lee Ann, 7, 26, 49
Wang, J., 52
Water crisis. *See* Flint water crisis
Watson, M., 9
Wells, Dr. Eden, 26
Wenger, E., 106
White supremacy, 19–20, 21, 141. *See ßalso* Racism
Whitlock, A. M., 71, 88, 104
Whitlock, Maggie, 6, 47–48, 60, 67–68, 75, 94–95
Whitlock, McKenzie, 60, 63–65, 72, 73
Whitmer, Governor Gretchen, 9
WIC (Women, Infants, and Children), 53
Williams, Roslyn, 79–80

Yosso, T. J., 105, 130

Zeichner, K., 106
Zoltowski, C. B., 55
Zygmunt, E., 105, 107, 123

About the Author

Annie McMahon Whitlock is an associate professor of history/social studies at Grand Valley State University in Allendale, Michigan. From 2013–2022, she was an Associate Professor at the University of Michigan-Flint, where she supervised student teachers, taught courses in both the elementary and secondary programs, and served as chair of the Education Department. Her research is centered on teaching elementary social studies through place-based inquiry, civic engagement, and curriculum integration. Her scholarship has been published in *Social Studies and the Young Learner*, *Journal of Social Studies Research*, and *The Social Studies*, among others. Dr. Whitlock was the inaugural editor of the peer-reviewed *Great Lakes Social Studies Journal*, a Michigan Council for the Social Studies publication, and is a member of their board of directors and a past member of the National Council for the Social Studies Board. Her most important roles are ones of wife, auntie, daughter, sister, and mom to humans Maggie and McKenzie and to her dog Barkley.